Electras

Electras
Aeschylus, Sophocles, and Euripides
Michael Davis

St. Augustine's Press
South Bend, Indiana

Manufactured in the United States of America.

1 2 3 4 5 6 28 27 26 25 24 23

Library of Congress Control Number: 2023944536

Paperback ISBN: 978-1-58731-208-3
Ebook ISBN: 978-1-58731-209-0

∞ The paper used in this publication meets the minimum
requirements of the American National Standard for Information Sciences –
Permanence of Paper for Printed Materials, ANSI Z39.48-1984.

St. Augustine's Press
www.staugustine.net

In memoriam—Seth Benardete

This is a book influenced throughout by the thought of the late Seth Benardete, an extraordinary scholar to be sure, but more important, a man of the greatest philosophical gifts. It is fair to say that my understandings of each of the three plays treated here are Benardetean; still, I have arrived at them in different ways. Benardete's written interpretation of the *Libation Bearers* in "On Greek Tragedy" is only a few pages long, but it is deep and rich.[1] It is at the heart of Chapter 1, where I have attempted to follow Benardete's lead closely, offering only my understanding of what I think he has already seen. I may, of course, have gotten him wrong, but the attempt has been to get his account right, spelling certain things out in more detail, but not diverging from the line of argument he has indicated. In the 1990's I attended a seminar that Benardete taught on Sophocles' *Electra*; I have since made ample use of his class notes. Over the years we had many conversations about the play. It is a great loss to us that he never wrote up his interpretation. Now, while it would be foolish to claim that Chapter 2 is the interpretation he would have written, it is an interpretation grounded in my understanding of what he had seen. Benardete and I never talked about Euripides' *Electra*, and so its interpretation in Chapter 3 is in some sense altogether my own. On the other hand, I begin with the sort of puzzles I imagine he would have posed and pursue them as I imagine he would have pursued them. Teachers affect us in many ways. In Chapter 1, I take my bearings from what Benardete wrote, in Chapter 2 from what he taught, and in Chapter 3 from how he taught. In this sense *Electras* is a thoroughly Benardetean book, but it is meant as a celebration of his thought, not a substitution for it. I do this proudly, all the while being humbled by the knowledge that it is not the book he would have written.

1   Benardete, Seth, "Chapter Seven: On Greek Tragedy" in *The Argument of the Action* (Chicago: University of Chicago Press, 2000) 123–26.

Contents

Introduction

> ". . . in the image of God He created it, male and female he created them."[2]

Man and woman, husband and wife—these are no longer matters that the educated elite of the academy are accustomed to discussing without suspicion. And yet they are the perennial beginning points for those from whom we have always sought education, those who ask themselves in a powerful way what it means to be human.[3] Regardless of present-day doubts about the relation between sex and gender and about the binary character of our understanding of sexuality, even in rejecting these terms as insufficient, in articulating the complexity that is thought to be lacking, poets, novelists, anthropologists, psychologists, and philosophers find it difficult to dispense with "man and woman," "husband and wife."[4] We may think ourselves to be escaping Plato's cave of conventional opinion when we insist on speaking of "pregnant persons," and indeed to speak in this way may shock us into wondering anew about the strangeness of

2   I have borrowed Ronna Burger's translation of Genesis 1.27. "It" could also read "him." For other translations, see https://biblia.com/bible/esv/genesis/1/26-27.

3   Consider, for example, the whole of Hesiod's *Theogony*, the relation between Egypt and Scythia in Herodotus's *History*, Plato's *Republic* Book 5, Aristotle's *Politics* Book 1, Canto 2 of Dante's *Inferno*, Rousseau's *Emile* Book 5, Goethe's *Faust*, and the first sentences of Austen's *Pride and Prejudice* and Nietzsche's *Beyond Good and Evil*.

4   This is true whether one intends to argue for sexual differences as natural or as constructed. See, for example, Levi-Strauss's *The Elementary Structures of Kinship*, Mead's *Coming of Age in Samoa*, de Beauvoir's *The Second Sex*, Irigaray's *Ethics of Sexual Difference*, not to mention Freud, Jung, Lacan, Foucault, and Butler. The list could, of course, be much, much longer.

1

what we ordinarily take to be quite ordinary—pregnancy. Still, with one difference, there is something Aristophanic in the new order that this terminology seeks to usher in—Aristophanes knew he was funny. While claiming to be a proclamation of our ascent from the cave to enlightenment, "pregnant person" seems rather a sign that we are digging ourselves deeper into darkness. There is something both revealing and funny about choosing one's own pronoun. It proclaims itself an act of freedom, but who exactly is it that does this choosing? Are human beings free in the sense that we begin from nothing? Is Entwerfen ever possible apart from Geworfenheit? Doesn't freedom take work? And if it is rather an end to be realized than a beginning to be taken for granted, isn't this work of freeing ourselves what used to be called liberal education?

Now, no doubt traditional liberal education always contains conventional doctrines—artifacts of the cave of Plato's *Republic* posing as truths of nature. And it is hard to distinguish the natural from the conventional. Because being in the cave of opinion means not knowing precisely which questions to pose, and since what seems most questionable is likely itself to be only conventionally so, as long as our interrogation is not too moralistic, questioning the obvious is likely to bear fruit. "Pregnant person" serves its purpose. Choosing one's pronoun reveals an indeterminacy in the being who chooses. Our education requires us to be open to anything, all the while being wary of being self-righteous, and thereby closed, in our openness. It requires that "one surrender to another while fighting every inch of the way"; this is hermeneutical moderation—"questioning the wisdom of the authority to which one defers."[5]

In our moral certainty, we run the risk of losing the "wisdom of the ancients." We carelessly think of the Greeks of the classical period as "dead white men" utterly formed by the customs of their time. They are, to be sure, dead, but "white" is a strange way to speak of them—as though they were of a piece with our acronym "WASP"—itself a problematic and conventional designation gobbling up groups of people to

---

5   Both quotations are from Seth Benardete's "Interpreting Plato's Charmides" in *The Argument of the Action* (Chicago: University of Chicago Press, 2000), 243.

which it was once defined in opposition. We might wonder as well about how a culture steeped in a doctrine of "white" male superiority could produce a prominent philosopher named Preserver-of-strength who was married to a woman named Yellow-horse, and in which the same male philosopher could explain his exemplary activity by likening it to weaving and midwifery, claim to know nothing except what he was taught by a female prophet, lay down as a principle of the best political order the equality of men and women, and learn oratory from Pericles' mistress (whom he also claims to be the true author of Pericles' funeral oration). Socrates was a gadfly, not a wasp. Greeks did not all think the same things and, as with us, their most famous "spokesmen" are perhaps the least likely among them to have thought what everyone else thought. Their great historians, philosophers, and poets may well have had something to do with the formation of future caves of opinion, but for that very reason, they were perhaps the least likely of their contemporaries to be captivated by and captives of their own cave.

Aeschylus, Sophocles and Euripides were Greeks of this sort. It is certainly true that Greek culture did not favor Greek women. All three poets knew this. They were not isolated intellectuals; they lived public lives, knew their world, and wrote about the world they knew. Aeschylus is said to have been proudest not of his poetry but of having fought for Athens at Marathon. Sophocles was a general and a friend of and counselor to Pericles. Euripides, whether a proto-feminist or a misogynist (both have been argued) was at the very least a well-known public intellectual. And yet the one, and by far the most impressive, character to appear in all three plays of Aeschylus's *Oresteia* (which constitutes three his seven extant plays) is Clytemnestra. In five of the seven plays we have of Sophocles, he presents formidable women in public settings (where their culture would never have allowed them to be). And of Euripides' eighteen extant plays, arguably fifteen either have powerful female roles or are concerned with themes having to do with women or both. Homer's *Iliad* may begin with the line, "Sing goddess the wrath of Peleus's son, Achilles," but even here in the poem at the very beginning of Greek culture, a poem about manliness and war, the Greeks go to war over a woman, Helen, and, by withdrawing from combat, Achilles goes to war with Agamemnon over a woman, Briseis.

Aeschylus, Sophocles, and Euripides would have understood the wonderful puzzle contained in ". . . in the image of God He created it, male and female he created them." There are two pieces to human beings that are at once at odds and yet always together. That the two are joined in different proportions differentiates us. Aeschylus, Sophocles, and Euripides understood the problematic doubleness of *anthrōpos*, human being, in terms of male and female. When we cannot resist the temptation to recoil morally from their terminology, we risk the tragedy of losing their profound thoughts about our humanity—their philosophical anthropology.

In the thirty-two extant Greek tragedies, one story alone is treated by all three of these poets—the story of Electra. Thinking through Aeschylus's *Libation Bearers* and the *Electra*s of Sophocles and Euripides offers a unique opportunity to learn deeply, on the one hand, about the meaning of the story itself—especially in connection with the power of the female, socially and politically to be sure, but perhaps more important, metaphysically—and, on the other, about the relation among the three playwrights and their different understandings of the female.

In outline, the Electra stories are more or less the same. Accompanied by Pylades, his cousin, Orestes returns home from long exile and is recognized by his sister, Electra. Together they mean to avenge the death of their father, Agamemnon, at the hands of their mother, Clytemnestra, and her new husband, Aegisthus. Each of the three plays is a story of matricide, of what might justify it, and of what it is that grounds our relations to mothers, fathers, and siblings. It is also the story of Electra's part, the female part, in the matricide, and, at least superficially, the playwrights seem to treat this quite differently. Electra disappears half-way through Aeschylus's *Libation Bearers*; she longs for an avenger, but plays no role in the killing of Clytemnestra by Orestes. And Aeschylus's play is not named for her. In Sophocles' *Electra*, Electra and Orestes do not meet until two-thirds of the way through the play, after the plan for revenge has already been set in motion. Electra has expressed her desire for revenge, but in the end, although she has been present on stage for virtually the whole play, she has very little to do with what happens. In Euripides' *Electra*, while Orestes kills both his mother and Aegisthus he is only his sister's instrument; she is the mastermind of the plan—the cause of the action.

It is not unusual to observe that Aeschylus, Sophocles, and Euripides are quite different dramatists. It is harder to say exactly what this means. A comparison of their Electras seems a fruitful place to begin, for each of them understood the female to be the deeper, if the less easily accessible and articulated, of the pair of fundamental principles constituting human beings.[6] This difficulty in articulation has led predictably to privileging what is straightforwardly sayable—the male trumps the female. Through their Electras, in different ways, Aeschylus, Sophocles, and Euripides go "beyond good and evil" to write about this problem of what is so powerful that it cannot be written.[7] Perhaps we can begin to understand what they are about and the differences between them by thinking through how they treat the same thing differently.

6   This ranking is not unlike Nietzsche's account the relation between the Dionysian and the Apollinian. See the whole of *The Birth of Tragedy* and my *The Music of Reason*, Part 2.

7   See the first sentence of the Preface of Friedrich Nietzsche's *Beyond Good and Evil*.

Chapter 1
Aeschylus: Electra Bound[8]

Puzzles[9]

Aeschylus writes the first of the three extant Greek tragedies dealing with the death of Clytemnestra at the hands of her children. Unlike the plays by Sophocles and Euripides, this one is called not *Electra* but *Choēphoroi—Libation Bearers*.[10] Why? Why instead does it take the

8   All translations from the Greek are my own and follow the text of the Oxford University Press editions of Aeschylus, Sophocles and Euripides.

9   Seth Benardete called my attention to most of the puzzles that follow. That my interpretation of the *Libation Bearers* amounts to working through these puzzles is a small indication of how deeply this chapter is indebted to Benardete. Dazzling though they are, he wrote only a few pages on the *Libation Bearers* (*Argument of the Action,* Chicago: University of Chicago Press, 2000, 173–76). The relation of the play to the rest of the *Oresteia* is clarified in his "Aeschylus' *Agamemnon*: The Education of the Chorus" in *The Archaeology of the Soul* (South Bend, IN: St. Augustine's Press, 2012), 41–57; and "The Furies of Aeschylus," 62–70, and "On Greek Tragedy," 99–145, both in *The Argument of the Action* (Chicago: University of Chicago Press, 2000). Benardete's course notes on the *Libation Bearers* are available at: https://digitalarchives.library.newschool.edu/index.php/ Browse/objects/facet/collection_facet/id/619. I have relied on all of these sources and on many private conversations with Benardete about the play. It is a hopeless task to indicate the extent of my indebtedness to his understanding of the *Libation Bearers*. Perhaps I should say that if something sounds smart, it is probably traceable back to him.

10   In Aristophanes' *Frogs* (1124), Euripides demands of Aeschylus that he speak the first lines of his *Oresteia*, and Aeschylus responds with the first lines of the *Libation Bearers*. Is this a mistake, or is the central play somehow meant to incorporate the elements of the whole trilogy? So, for example, the first play begins with a reference to the cosmic gods, and the third

name of the chorus of slave women taken captive (75–78) one imagines from Troy?[11] Why on earth should they side with Electra over Clytemnestra in order to avenge the man who killed their relatives and sacked their city? The title of Aeschylus's play, then, makes it immediately apparent that, however smoothly the story may seem to unfold, we don't really understand what is going on.

A brief glance at the plot will confirm this knowledge of ignorance. As the play opens, Orestes has returned from Phocis, where he has been in exile (we do not know for how long), to his home, Argos. He is accompanied by his friend and cousin Pylades, who is surely one of the strangest figures in all of Greek tragedy. Pylades has only one line in the play, but what a line it is, for when Orestes expresses some doubt about killing his mother, Pylades tells him to follow the oracle and kill her (899–902).[12] In the prologue, the two stand before the tomb of Agamemnon, where they place two locks of hair from Orestes as an offering. The tomb stands before the palace and is large enough for two grown men to hide behind. Since Argos is now ruled by those who hated Agamemnon, we wonder why his burial place is so prominent.

In the parodos, the chorus and Electra approach and are clearly in mourning, but Orestes notices that the chorus are just going through the motions and identifies Electra as the only genuine mourner (17–18; see also 82–84). Electra arrives and prays for Orestes to return and for an avenger to appear (she does not connect the two). Discovering the locks of hair she assumes, because they are very like her hair, that they could only come from Orestes, and then concludes that he must have sent them and therefore will not come himself. Accordingly, she despairs. But then she notices two sets of footprints. As one set is very like hers, she assumes they must belong to Orestes, and therefore he must indeed be in Argos. At this very moment, Orestes emerges from behind the tomb and announces himself. We wonder why he waited so long, and wonder as well why

with a reference to Earth. Chthonic Hermes, the psychopomp, the god with whom the *Libation Bearers* begins, is somehow an intermediary between the two.

11   Their Asian origins are made clear at 160–63 and 423.

12   In the plays of Sophocles and Euripides, he does not speak at all.

Electra, who has just convinced herself that he is at hand, does not believe that the man she sees (hair and feet intact) is Orestes. In the end, she is convinced only by his possession of a piece of her own weaving (weaving which is, of course, rather more transferable than feet, or even hair).

Orestes then tells of an oracle he has received from Apollo, which he takes to command him to kill his mother (although he doesn't call her that until he turns to Pylades at 899 to ask whether he should kill her), but when he repeats the oracle, it proves to be conditional and not a categorical command, and so it is not clear that he has actually been told to kill his mother, but rather what he will suffer if he does not. And yet, oddly, the suffering he describes does not differ much from what, having killed her, he ends up enduring anyway (273–76).

At this point there is a long *kommos* where, for reasons that are not immediately clear, Orestes, Electra, and the chorus attempt to call Agamemnon back from the dead. While they fail, their failure doesn't really seem to change anything. The chorus then tell why Clytemnestra has sent them to propitiate the dead Agamemnon—apparently, she was frightened by a dream in which she suckled a snake, which drew blood from her breast. Orestes reinterprets the dream (in a rather obvious way) so that not Agamemnon, but he, is the snake.

He then reveals his plan for vengeance, such as it is, in which neither Electra nor the chorus are to play a role, suggesting that, had her inference from the footprints not revealed his presence, Orestes might have never have involved Electra at all. But why exclude her? The plan—he and Pylades will hang around the gates of the palace speaking in a Phocian dialect until, given their status as *xenoi* (strangers), Aegisthus, shamed by the law of *xenia* (guest-friendship), admits them, at which point Orestes will kill him (later, for reasons that are never made clear, Orestes will alter the plan and announce that they bring word from Phocis about Orestes). Killing in this way certainly more than qualifies as a violation of the law of *xenia*. Agamemnon, we remember, prosecuted the Trojan War because Paris's theft of Helen violated this law. The chorus then sing an ode about a series of mythic murders of kin—none particularly apt and none a matricide—after which Orestes sets his plan in motion.

In a curiously comic scene, Orestes knocks on the door and yells "Boy! Boy!", receiving a reply from offstage (something otherwise unexampled in Greek tragedy where we sometimes hear voices from offstage, but never in conversation with those onstage). After this, the tone of the play changes markedly. Its language is less lush and more matter of fact. Orestes' former nurse is sent by Clytemnestra to summon Aegisthus and his guards. Happening to intercept her, the chorus tell her to cancel the guards. Since, if the chorus had not done so, Orestes and Pylades would have been killed, the success of the plan depends on the accidental intervention of the chorus and the nurse.

As instructed (albeit only hypothetically), Orestes kills Aegisthus without revealing who he is—i.e., "after the same fashion" (274) as Agamemnon had been killed. He then confronts Clytemnestra as "mother" for the first time (in this case not following Apollo's instructions), asks Pylades what to do, and then kills her. After this, the chorus sing in a triumphant meter (the dochmiacs used in the *Eumenides*). Pointing to the bloody net or cloth used in the killing of Agamemnon, Orestes justifies the murder of his mother, but is nevertheless beset by furies, seen only by him. He says he is going mad and runs off. The chorus conclude the play by rehearsing the fates of Thyestes and Agamemnon, and then adding Orestes to the list.

Of the many puzzling details and unsettling questions in the play, perhaps the greatest is that no later than line 509 Electra disappears, and the chorus and the nurse take the role that she might have had as Orestes' co-conspirator. Since she is so easily removed from the play, we wonder why it is necessary for her to be present at all. Or, put somewhat differently, when Sophocles and Euripides tell this story they do so in plays named *Electra*. Why is this not true of Aeschylus? Or, still differently, while Electra is clearly necessary for the recognition scene, why is this scene, the details of which Euripides finds so easy to ridicule (*Electra* 508–46), necessary? Let us turn to the beginning of the play to try to unravel some of these knots.

The Prologue and Parados (1–83)

The first five lines of the *Libation Bearers* contain a series of ambiguities. Orestes calls upon chthonic Hermes who looks over the rule of the father. Who is the father in question? Agamemnon? Zeus? Does Orestes request a savior/preserver for him who is praying, or for him making a claim to a patrimony? Is Orestes returning to the land or descending to the land? And what is the difference between asking the father to hear (*kluein*) and to listen (*akousai*)? Why are these *logoi* so indeterminate? Then there is the tomb, another ambiguous sign. Do its size and prominence mean that Clytemnestra and Aegisthus are throwing Agamemnon's murder in the face of the Argives, or does it indicate their regret?

Orestes leaves two locks of hair—one indicating gratitude, one indicating grief (6), but absent his explanation, the two look identical. That by themselves they are meaningless, that they require interpretation, is connected to a further ambiguity. In the extant Greek tragedies, the *Libation Bearers* is the only play in which Hades is not mentioned. What is the relation between the corpse that Orestes was not present to touch (8–9) and the one before which he is now present? To whom exactly is Orestes speaking?[13]

As the chorus of libation bearers approach, Orestes sees, or thinks he sees, that in contrast to Electra, they do not feel real grief. He wonders what *chrēma*, what thing of use, he sees (10). The chorus may be conspicuous (*prepousa*—12) in their black robes, but Electra is "conspicuous" (19) in her bitter grief. Orestes guesses (*proseikassō*—12) that this means Electra's grief is authentic while theirs is perfunctory. The comparison is more complicated than it seems, for in the parados (75–83) the chorus will appear to feel real grief, concealed however because it is not Agamemnon for whom they mourn. So, we have three levels of grief—genuine, conventional, and genuine concealed as conventional. How are we to tell them apart?

And why do we need Pylades? A ritual procession, which by its very nature assumes that there is some being there to appease, turns out to be addressed not to Agamemnon, but to two men hiding behind a tomb. One is Orestes come home. One is a virtually anonymous man whose

---

13 While the *kommos* will be addressed to Agamemnon (presumably to convince him to return from the dead), neither Orestes nor Electra, but only the chorus (372–79) seem to acknowledge that this requires a place like Hades, where Agamemnon still exists. As a result, it is never really clear whom they are addressing when they speak to Agamemnon.

sole line in the play might be abbreviated to say, "Kill her!" The two are addressed in two ways—the chorus only ritually and Electra really meaning it. In this first scene then, Orestes is not the only one forced to guess or infer through likenesses.

The parados (22–83) divides into three strophic systems and an epode. In the first strophe (22–31), the chorus describe themselves. They are conspicuous (*prepei*—24) for their blood red cheeks. So, their black clothing is conspicuous—a sign of mourning—but what covers the body is not really what is at stake. A sign of mourning is not mourning. And so, their clothing is torn to expose what lies beneath it, their bodies, but the body revealed in these tears is not really what is at stake. And so the body, in turn, is torn, leaving the red blood within it conspicuous, but blood is not really what is at stake.[14] While the grief of Electra is conspicuous, Electra is not simply her grief. The parados begins by seemingly moving us progressively from outer manifestations to inner truths, but the "inner" always falls short as it reveals itself as a new "outer."

This problem is confirmed in the first antistrophe (32–41). Depending on how one reads line 32, either fear (*phobos*) or Apollo (*Phoibos*) cried out (*elake*) from the innermost quarters of the house, the women's chambers—this is presumably actually Clytemnestra's response to her dream. Only a few lines later (38), using the same verb, the interpreters are said to have cried out their interpretation of the dream. When the verb *laskein* is used of human beings it certainly can mean "to cry out," but it is used more often of inanimate objects to mean "to ring or crash" and of animals to mean "to bay or howl." Aeschylus thus uses language here that by emphasizing the sound of the outcry, brings to the fore the doubleness of the verb *legein* as both "to speak" and "to mean." It calls our attention to the fact that external sound is not equivalent to inner meaning. And inner meaning is the ever-elusive result of interpreting what is external and available.

Despite this ambiguity, when the judges cry out, their interpretation is assured by the gods (38). But what is this judgment that the gods guarantee? —that those below the earth are angry at the killers (39–41).

---

14 And, of course, while the cheeks of the chorus are red from mourning, are they mourning Agamemnon, or are they mourning their own dead?

These are the first of many instances in the play of what seem to be poetic plurals—plural in form, but meant to be singular in meaning. The problem, however, is that, because here, and throughout the *Libation Bearers*, these plurals may or may not be poetic, it is not possible to be sure what they mean. If both "those beneath the earth" and "killers" are taken as singular, then the antistrophe would probably be saying that Agamemnon was angry at Clytemnestra. If the first is singular and the second a normal plural, then Agamemnon would be angry at Clytemnestra and Aegisthus. If both were normal plurals, it could mean that in general the shades in Hades are angry at the two killers. Or if the latter were taken as a singular, it might mean their anger is reserved for Clytemnestra. Since the overriding issue of the *Oresteia* is justice, it would seem rather important to know who is blaming and who is being blamed. As is regularly the case with divine oracles, the gods' guarantee here is deceptively ambiguous.

The second strophic system (42–65) continues this pattern. In the strophe (42–53) the chorus express their fear. They don't want to pour libations offensive to the earth, libations as atonement (*lutron*) for blood falling to the ground (48); they fear as well that the word they throw out will offend (47). Ordinarily *lutron* would mean not "atonement" but "ransom." And the plurals at lines 50, 52, and 53 could be read to mean that the chorus lament the darkness that shrouds the houses and masters of both Argos and Troy. Are they afraid here of Agamemnon's wrath or of the wrath of their own dead for pouring libations for the man who ravaged their homeland?

The antistrophe (54–65) confirms this ambiguity. If "good fortune is among mortals a god and more than a god" (59–60), it involves luck—more than is reasonably predictable. Why? Good fortune requires justice, but blood spilled cannot be unspilled—there is never a perfect tit for tat, no eye for an eye because time does not heal wounds. Daylight may bring the quick justice (61–62) of an altogether intelligible order, but we do not live in the perfect enlightenment of the day. We live either in the shadows, where a murky, late justice that might prevail in the end does not prevent our having suffered from the delay (this is Electra's life), or in utter darkness (65), with no intelligible order and without any justice at all (they fear that this is to be their fate).

The third strophic system (66–74) echoes this problem. The strophe (66–70) uses a series of words that may imply action, and so inner intent, and may simply register external events (66–67, 70) to conclude that the bloodstain of injustice is indelible. The antistrophe (71–74) tells us why. What is done cannot be undone. The past transforms the once voluntary into the involuntary—the possible into the necessary. As no restoration is possible, no payment, atonement, or cure is possible. In the most extreme of crimes especially, rape and murder, there is no possible return to the *status quo ante*. Innocence lost is not to be recovered.

This general point is driven home in the concluding epode (75–78). Justice is not possible so long as a crime cannot be undone. Since behind the desire to punish is always a hopeless attempt to regain innocence, it is not justifiable to kill Clytemnestra in the belief that her death will restore piety—the ancestral regime. This will be the key to the *Libation Bearers* as a whole. Justice is possible only when the good of the avenger, his self-interest. is simply just. And here, this would require that Agamemnon avenge his own death, and so, either Agamemnon must be brought back to life or Orestes must become Agamemnon. In the *kommos*, Orestes and Electra fail to restore Agamemnon to life, and of course if they could, the crime of Clytemnestra would not be as serious as it is. What then might be possible? If there were a being extending through all time and against which all crimes were thought to be committed, it could serve as the instrument of its own revenge. The epode first suggests and then discards the possibility that the *polis*, the city, is such a being.[15] Only in the city is there an identity between father and son as rulers— "the king is dead; long live the king."[16] And yet the chorus themselves serve as the sign that the immortality of the city is an illusion, for their city has been destroyed and their vengeance denied. Accordingly, the fear that characterizes Clytemnestra in the first antistrophe, and the chorus pouring libations in the second strophe, is generalized by the chorus in the second antistrophe as the universal condition of mortals.

15 This possibility is the theme of the *Eumenides*.
16 See 500–09.

Electra and Orestes: Episode One (84–305)

The first episode begins with Electra asking the chorus for advice.[17] She knows what she must do, but not what she should say. The issue is the significance of what she will do. Electra could say that she brings libations from "one loving to one loved," but that would be false, and Electra is reluctant to lie about Clytemnestra. She might simply say what is customary and ask that the libations be rewarded with what is deserved—keeping her reluctance tacit. Or, she might say nothing and let the libations speak for themselves. Electra thus asks the chorus whether her deed should be precise (utterly in the light of *logos*), ambiguous (only partially lit by *logos*, and so in the shadows), or silent altogether (and so in utter darkness). The problem is that precise speech leads to injustice, and silence means making no request whatsoever and so leaving the meaning of the libations completely to the gods so that she contributes not at all to the working of justice. Ambiguity is somehow Electra's only viable option. Her deed must speak and yet not speak. Actions by themselves, supposing they are even possible, never suffice—they are meaningless unless accompanied by *logoi*. But from the very beginning of the play, we have seen that *logoi* too admit of ambiguity, and must do so lest they be overly precise—lies. Accordingly, Electra asks of her father that Orestes return (130–31) and that an avenger come to do justice and kill Agamemnon's killers (141–43). This may be a poetic plural and so not necessarily involve the death of her mother, but Electra never indicates that the two requests will be satisfied by one person. Her *logos* is ambiguous about who will be killed and ambiguous about who will do the killing. Electra longs for vengeance, but it is not clear that she is willing to do what is required to enact it.[18] Her speech indicates that Orestes has multiple selfish motives to return to Argos (135–38),

---

17 Electra first addresses them as *dmōmai* (84)—female slaves—and asks their advice, although she soon call them friends (*philoi*—100). At 103–04 she will suggest that they are potentially her equals, since both free and slave in the end meet with the same fate. Still, while she claims at 109–16 that she will ask favor for them as well as herself, at 130–31 she seems to forget about them altogether—after all, they are just slaves.

18 This reluctance will be thematic in Sophocles' treatment of Electra.

and Electra is hard-pressed to articulate an unambiguously just motive for revenge. Because she cannot both preserve her innocence and act, she can take no part in the plot and must drop out of the play.

Thus far the *Libation Bearers* has repeatedly brought to the surface two fundamental problems. The first is the emptiness of outer signs apart from an inner meaning, whether these signs are taken to be things, deeds, or *logoi*. The second is that when justice is understood as paying back what is owed, if this pay-back unfolds in time, it must necessarily be imperfect. The one comes to a head in the recognition scene (164–305), where we are forced to ask what constitutes a proof of identity. The other is the issue of the attempt to call Agamemnon back from the dead in the great *kommos* that substitutes for the first stasimon (306–478).

As the recognition scene begins, Electra has just finished pouring libations. Accordingly, she must be in front of Agamemnon's tomb on the side opposite where Orestes and Pylades are hiding. She has just prayed for Orestes to return. He might have shown himself now, but waits until line 211. We have speculated that this may be because he did not want to show himself at all, but why would that be the case? Perhaps, obedient to Apollo, he wished his vengeance to be altogether anonymous. A certain anonymity is, after all, a feature of justice—the hangman wears a hood, and in statues, Justice is portrayed wearing a blindfold. Still, Orestes wishes to justify himself and therefore has to emerge as Orestes. He wants to get credit for having been an anonymous instrument of justice.[19]

Seeing the locks of hair on the tomb, Electra turns to the chorus and says, "Share this new *muthos* with me" (166). She sees the hair not as a dumb thing, but as a *muthos*—a word or story; it is for her significant. Only a little later she adds "there is no one other than I who would have cut it" (171). Of course, she did not cut it. Her solution to this dilemma seems to be lines 175–80 where she first identifies the hair as Orestes' and then concludes that, since it would have been too fearsome for him

---

19 Compare Odysseus's frustration at not being recognized for his power to appear as other than he is throughout the *Odyssey*. It is the fate of the man of many ways, the *polutropos*, to show his power only by appearing in one way.

to come to Argos, he must have sent the hair. The strangest line is the compendious comparison at line 176— "It is very like our own selves to look upon." The language suggests a total identification of Orestes with Electra—where to be like something is to be that thing—simile turns into metaphor. There are two sorts of accounts here. In the first, a lock is discovered that is like Electra's hair. She makes it identical to her hair and then makes Orestes identical to herself. In the second, she asks who would place such a lock on the tomb, and since it was not she, would not be Clytemnestra, and no one else would do it, she concludes (with a nudge from the chorus) that it must have been Orestes. But Electra treats the two arguments as though they were the same. She seems to think that she needs evidence like the lock—a solid thing—that nails down her conclusion independent of any intervening interpretation. But her language betrays her, for she refers to the lock as a *muthos*, a story or word—indicating that she is building a scenario (Orestes sent the lock) around "evidence" that is not at all evident without a prior scenario (no one but Orestes would have sent it). It is particularly strange that Electra should collapse these two modes of argument here since the chorus simply ignore the likeness of looks, and in her long speech, she too drops it altogether until it returns with her discovery of footprints around the tomb. The inferential character of this "evidence" is brought into relief by the fact that Electra infers wrongly—Orestes is indeed in Argos.

However, before she discovers the footprints, Electra makes a series of dubious inferences—that because no one in the city is on the side of Agamemnon (how does she know this?), none other than she, Orestes, or Clytemnestra could be "master of this curl" (*phobē*, or, if one reads the pun, "master of this fear"—*phobos*); that the hair cannot have come from Clytemnestra who has an "ungodly spirit" toward her children (Electra ignores Iphigenia); and that Clytemnestra hates her (it does not occur to her that, while Clytemnestra killed Agamemnon out of hatred, the suffering of Electra, although the result of Clytemnestra's action is not the intent of her action—for Electra, this outside seems to provide perfect access to Clytemnestra's inside). Electra sees that the problem is that the hair is mute—"Would that it had a gracious voice, like (*dikēn*) a messenger" (195), but if *dikēn* is taken, as is more usual, as the noun "right" or "justice," she might be saying "Would that it had a graceful voice of a messenger with respect to justice."[20] Later the muteness of hair will allow Orestes to enter the house without revealing his identity—it will enable a deception. Here, Electra regrets her inability to appeal to a bare fact as though to a messenger with a *logos* but, of course, *logos* too is not univocal. Now, having just ignored the two locks and called them one, Electra discovers a second sign, which is also two—the footprints.

Electra looks at the imprint of Orestes' foot and finds them "like to" and "resembling" hers (206), the heels and tendons, when measured, agreeing with hers (210). One doesn't need Euripides' parody of this scene in his *Electra* (508–46) to see how wobbly this is as a principle of identification. That a man's footprint should be identical to his sister's is no more plausible than that his hair should be a match for hers. Furthermore, Electra herself does not seem particularly convinced by her conclusion. Although she has just inferred that since Orestes' footprint is present, he himself must be present, when Orestes emerges from behind the tomb and identifies himself, she refuses to believe him. We often speak of experiences that could simply confirm the truth of our speech, but does any experience really have this sort of directness or immediacy? The lock of hair is mute. The footprint, of course, differs from

20 For this ambiguity with respect to *dikēn* as a noun and as a preposition see Seth Benardete, "The Furies of Aeschylus" and "On Greek Tragedy" in *The Argument of the Action* (Chicago: University of Chicago Press, 2000), 62, 124. In his seminar Benardete pointed out that the prepositional use of *dikēn* occurs more in the *Oresteia* than in the rest of extant Greek literature combined (twenty times) and more than twice as many times in the *Agamemnon* (fourteen) than in the other two plays of the trilogy (three in the *Libation Bearers* and three in the *Eumenides*). The point is that "the exaction of right has given way to the inexactness of simile" ("The Furies of Aeschylus," 62). The chorus report that in her dream Clytemnestra says that she anchored the snake like (*dikēn*) a child in swaddling clothes. Benardete points out that if we read *dikēn* not as a preposition but as the accusative singular of "justice," the chorus "could possibly mean that in the swaddling clothes of a child she anchored just punishment. The child, then would not be Orestes but Iphigenia, and the interpreters would have told Clytemnestra that the sacrifice of Iphigenia does not now sanction her father's murder." ("On Greek Tragedy," 124).

the hair. As a piece of Orestes, detachable from him as a whole, the hair is not certainly identifiable as belonging to Orestes. It is independent— like a child cut off from its mother. The footprint is a sign of a part of Orestes not severed from the whole of him. Still, it is a sign and, while perhaps like Orestes' foot, it is not identical to his foot. The authenticity of both signs, the hair and the footprint, is mediated through Electra.

What do we actually know at the end of this recognition scene? The two locks of hair belong to the man who claims to be Orestes. The hair is like, even very like, Electra's. The man's footprints are like Electra's. He has a piece of embroidery sewn by Electra. But none of this is enough. The sign of the overall problem emerges when we compare line 220, where Electra asks Orestes, "What snare, stranger, are you weaving (*plekeis*) about me?" and line 231, where Orestes calls upon Electra to look at the woven robe (*huphasma*), the work of her hand, with line 187, where, discovering the locks, Electra says, "Look at the lock/woven hair/*plokamon*." Is even hair an artifice?

The recognition scene places enormous emphasis on the identity of the external features of Orestes and Electra, and then on the identity of Orestes and Electra.

> Orestes: You have come into the sight of what you long prayed for.
> Electra: And among mortals whom do you know along with me that I call for?
> Orestes: Along with you I know that you admire Orestes greatly.
> Electra: Toward what then have I prayed earnestly?
> Orestes: I am he. Do not seek for him more dear than I.
> Electra: What snare, stranger, are you weaving about me?
> Orestes: I myself, with respect to myself, then, am devising.
> Electra: But do you wish to laugh at my ills?
> Orestes: Of mine too, then, if indeed at yours.
>
> 214–23

After showing Electra the embroidery she once wove, Orestes warns her to contain herself, literally to "come to be within" and not to be "knocked out of her wits by joy" (233). She will discover his identity so long as she does not lose her own or, put differently, Electra wishes to be as certain of Orestes' identity as she is of her own. In each case, what convinces her is something that brings her back to herself. To know with the certainty with which one knows oneself is somehow *the* measure of evidence.

This is connected to Electra's speech at 235–45.

Most dear darling of your father's house,
wept over hope of the preserving seed,
having persuaded by force you will recover your father's house.
Joyful vision having four proper parts
for me—to speak of (or: address) you necessarily as
father, and from me to you falls the affection accorded to the mother,
she who is in all justice hated
and of the same-seed (or: sister) sacrificed without mercy,
and, as brother, you were trust.
[you] alone bearing my reverence.
Would that both Might and Right,
with Zeus, greatest of all, as a third come to be with you.

So, Electra imagines that Orestes will recover his father's house—he will restore the situation that existed before the death of Agamemnon. But what would this involve? If he could somehow be a complete substitute for all those lost in her family, Orestes would with one blow restore family harmony. As it is, Electra cannot love Agamemnon because he sacrificed Iphigenia. She cannot love Clytemnestra because she killed Agamemnon. And should Orestes, acting simply as her brother, kill her mother, she would be unable to love him. To fulfill Electra's imagined goal, Orestes would have to be something other than her brother. Using the imperfect past tense at line 443, Electra says to him, "as brother, you were trust." Is he any longer her brother, or does her expression of his universal role as kin as such—at once, father, mother, sister, and brother—pave the way for removing him as brother so as not to skew his role as avenger? Or, is the point of putting Orestes in the role of simply *philtatos*—dearest, most loved or loving, most kindred—what is necessary in order to make him an avenger both powerful and concerned?[21]

21 At line 244, Zeus is "greatest of all" because a combination of Might and Right.

This idealizing of Orestes continues in the sequel, but rather as king than kin, and this time Orestes is its author. Like Agamemnon at Aulis, kings are said to serve as means to make the will of Zeus known. Will doesn't simply show itself; it must be interpreted. Because signs are always ambiguous, an instrument of interpretation, something like government, the *polis*, is necessary. Ironically, addressing Zeus, Orestes makes this claim about the necessity of the interpretive role of kingship in a metaphor, a speech itself requiring interpretation. Kings are eagles, Orestes an offspring of an eagle, and "once destroying an eagle's offspring, you would in turn not be able to send well trusted signs to mortals" (258–59). It seems not to occur to Orestes that Zeus too is a king, and so even the source of the sign is a sign requiring interpretation.

This revelation of the indeterminacy of signs from the gods is an apt introduction to Orestes' long speech about the meaning of the oracle he received from Apollo (269–305).[22] We learn several things. It is not at all clear whom Apollo has told Orestes to kill. In fact, it is not even clear Apollo has told Orestes to kill anyone. He only tells him what will happen if he does "not have a share in killing in return those responsible for the father" (273–74). To be sure, Orestes interprets this to mean Apollo wants him to kill Clytemnestra. So, for example, he interprets leprosy as the punishment he will incur for disobedience. But by itself leprosy is only an illness. To be understood as punishment, it must have a context. It must be embedded in a story—a *muthos*. The sign of this problem is that until line 284 Orestes speaks in indirect discourse. We are told that Apollo said these things, but, as we do not know Apollo's precise words, what we hear is Orestes' interpretation of their meaning. In the sequel (285–305), which seems to be in direct discourse, Orestes, now speaking in his own name, tells us that if he does not take vengeance, the dead will punish him with guilt. Strictly speaking then, guilt is the only punishment Orestes suffers. It consists not in the bare facts, but in

---

22 The speech follows the chorus's warning to Orestes and Electra to beware of "those in power." Now, on the one hand, this clearly refers to Clytemnestra and Aegisthus. Still, it might simply be a warning about all those in power. This would point to the deep ambiguity of the motives of the characters for whom this play is named.

the interpretation Orestes places on them—their significance in his tale, his *muthos*.

Put somewhat differently, Orestes ends his speech with an account of why he must be persuaded by the oracle:

> For many desires fall together into one,
> a command of a god and a great sorrow of/for a father,
> and a want of goods presses against [me]
> not to doom the most glorious citizens of mortals,
> destroyers of Troy, with hearts well renown,
> thus to be subjects to a pair of women.
> For female is his heart, and if not, it will be known to him soon.
>   297–305

Three things come together to move Orestes to act. The first two seem clear—his fear, which he represents as fear of disobeying the god, and his desire for gain, which he represents as longing, for the sake of the citizens of Argos, to restore his line to the throne (although this move requires considerable "interpretation" and a certain willful ignorance, since we know that the citizens do not really take his part, and to justify himself, Orestes must turn Aegisthus into a "woman," and claiming, Helen and the Trojan War to the contrary notwithstanding, that Greeks are not subject to women). The third motive, however, is less clear. What exactly is it that transforms grief for the father into intending to kill Clytemnestra? Is Orestes' real motive somehow the need to kill *the* mother, and if so, what does this signify? Any interpretation of the *Libation Bearers* will ultimately turn on how we understand the mother as a principle.

The Great Kommos: *306–478*

If there is an "ordinarily," ordinarily Greek tragedy begins with a prologue, followed by the parodos in which the chorus enter, followed by the first episode of the drama, followed by the first stasimon—an ode where the chorus sing and dance "in place." In the *Libation Bearers*, the first stasimon is replaced by a *kommos* (often called the Great *Kommos*), the purpose of which seems to be to raise Agamemnon from the dead. Here, the chorus sing from the orchestra not alone but rather in exchanges with Orestes and Electra, who are on stage in front of the stage wall, the *skēne*. The chorus begin by announcing the principle of justice.[23]

> "In return for hateful language let hateful
> language be fulfilled," with a great shout,
> Justice, enacting what is owed.
> "In return for bloody blow, let bloody
> blow be paid." For the one doing to suffer—
> these things a thrice old myth intones.
>
> 309–14

This emphasis on the distinction between speech and deed is repeated when Orestes replies and, addressing Agamemnon, asks what he can say or do to recall his father from the dead (316–17). Electra echoes this emphasis on speech and deed: "Or by saying what, would we happen upon the pains we suffered from those begetting [us]?" (418–19).[24] Shortly after, the chorus sing, "I beat an Arian beating/lamentation (*kommos*) in the custom of the wailing Kissian women . . . ." (423). Their words are wonderfully ambiguous. On the one hand, they are a lamentation; on the other, they are cleverly self-reflexive. The chorus utter a *kommos* in a tragedy; they do not enact a lamentation about an action, but "act" out a speech about such a lamentation. And so, here they too call our attention to the distinction between speech or significance, and deed or action.[25]

---

23 Here, for the first time in the trilogy, the word for justice is not *dikē* but the more prosaic *dikaion*.

24 The poetic plural of "those begetting" is interesting. Does Electra mean only her mother, or does she, whether wittingly or no, include her father?

25 Furthermore, "I beat (*koptō*)" is in the aorist tense. So, while they may be singing about Agamemnon, not only is its form, *kommos*, ambiguous but, as in the parodos, so too is its content. They may well be recalling their lamentation for their own dead, and so, all the talk of the crime of Agamemnon's burial, the mutilation of his corpse, may simply be a reminder of the burial rites they were prevented from performing. This possibility is sug-

The *kommos* has three parts. The first (306–404) consists of three strophic systems in mainly Aeolic meter, here rather ornate, sandwiched between verses in anapest—a marching meter indicating movement. The second part (405–55) consists of three strophic systems with no separation by verses in anapest. The meter is iambic—the meter of ordinary speech. The *kommos* then concludes with iambic verses (456–78).[26] There is some dispute about who utters these final lines, but let us assume they belong to the chorus. In moving from the more to less active, and from the more ornate to the more ordinary, the *kommos* seems to echo the movement of the *Libation Bearers*, and indeed of the whole of the *Oresteia*. Is it, then, in some way meant to be a microcosm of the whole—gradually replacing the movement of deed by the relative stasis of speech?

This formal division is duplicated on the level of content of the *kommos*. In the first strophic system of part one (306–44), we are given Agamemnon beneath the ground—his status altogether ambiguous. This ambiguity might easily lead to a tension between the views of the chorus and Orestes and Electra, or between the views of Electra and Orestes, for trying to recall Agamemnon from the dead should lead to the question of the possibility of a soul in the underworld, in Hades. Furthermore, with the failure to restore Agamemnon, the question of who will act to avenge him should be prominent. But in the first part of the *kommos*, the views of the chorus, Orestes, and Electra on these issues are artfully interlaced so as to finesse any possible differences. Only the chorus seem to realize that to bring Agamemnon joy by way of lamentation must mean that he still has mind or thought. While this implies the existence of something like a place where Agamemnon exists, Hades, with something like a soul, the chorus never make this explicit.

In the second strophic system (345–79) we are given the murder of Agamemnon. Here the views of Orestes and Electra begin to diverge from those of the chorus. Orestes claims there would be no cause for

gested as well by the fact that they say their lamentation conforms to Kissian, i.e., Asian, *nomoi*—customs or laws.

26 Here I am following Seth Benardete's analysis of the meter presented in his course on the *Libation Bearers*.

lamentation had Agamemnon died at Troy in battle. The chorus, who we must think are Trojan slaves, reply that Agamemnon is "dear to those dear to him" (354). They do not mention Troy at all and do not indicate that Agamemnon is one to whom they are dear. Electra then lapses into a sort of pure fantasy, imagining that Agamemnon did not die at Troy (363–64) at all, and that his "killers" nevertheless were punished in advance so as to die as he would have—that is, they suffered the fate Orestes has given Agamemnon in his previous speech, although she has just denied that Agamemnon suffered it. Electra wants to make their lamentation into an unlimited song of praise, but to do so she must sing of the triumph of justice, which in turn would mean making Agamemnon's death unlamentable, and require erasing its evil so thoroughly as to completely undo the evilness of the deed. Yet this would make her imagined punishment of the evildoers altogether unintelligible.

In the third strophic system (380–404), ignoring this difficulty, Orestes takes back Electra's pipe dream and claims that though the vengeance may come late (383), the debt to the parents (385) will be repaid. His poetic plural ("parents") leaves us wondering whether he owes a debt to Clytemnestra as well. The chorus's reply is hard to make out. To sing out when the man is struck down, and the woman (387–97), most obviously refers to Aegisthus and Clytemnestra, but could it not also once again refer to Agamemnon, who ravaged their homeland? Electra's final contribution to the first part is to say first that this vengeance will be inflicted by Zeus and then to ask for assurances that justice will be done from their land or place (*khōra*), from earth (*gē*), and from the underworlds (*kthonioi*). She combines an appeal to the Olympian gods with an appeal to the chthonic gods. So, the chorus never unambiguously identify Agamemnon as good and thereby worthy of revenge, Electra never identifies Orestes the agent of their revenge, and, while the chorus seem to appeal to the underworld as a reality, Orestes and Electra never invoke Hades. The first part of the Great *Kommos* thus allows the three to form an alliance by glossing over the serious differences that separate them, although still hinting at them in the process.

This glossing over becomes less possible in the second part (405–55). Here, Orestes asks Zeus what to do, and Electra asks what word to speak. The ignobility of the treatment of Agamemnon's corpse becomes an issue. Electra makes clear that she did not witness the deed, the actual mutilation of Agamemnon's body, and asks the chorus to hear and write in their hearts that she was locked away in her room. Orestes finally affirms his role as avenger, as actor; to be sure, vengeance is still attributed to divine powers, but it is effected by means of Orestes' hands (436–37). As ambiguities begin to disappear, differences come to be apparent. Electra, for whom revenge seems to exist primarily in speech, will soon disappear altogether from the play. After the *kommos* concludes Orestes says, "Father who died in a way not kingly (or: tyrannical), asked by me for the power of your house" (479–80). He seems not so much concerned with the fact of Agamemnon's death or with the question of whether his soul continues as with the mutilation of his body. It is somehow the significance of the mutilation of Agamemnon's body that forces Orestes' hand. Is the assertion that the father is a nobody, nothing (and so, of course, not a soul in Hades) what moves Orestes to decide to kill the mother?

The action of the *Libation Bearers*, like the Oresteia as a whole, marks a separation of Olympian from chthonic gods.[27] Orestes begins the play with mixed motives. He cannot know he will kill his mother at the start because he does not yet know what the result will be of the *kommos*. Will Agamemnon respond to their plea? Once this is settled, Orestes interprets Clytemnestra's dream. Agamemnon will not return to serve as a chthonic avenger, and so Orestes must be the serpent in the dream. The elimination of the chthonic leads directly to matricide. This movement coincides with the disappearance of Electra from the play. Does invoking the father have as its inner truth the elimination of the mother and of women generally?[28] The emergence of the Olympian gods

27 Each of the plays begins with the status of the pre-Olympian gods. Consider *Agamemnon* 1–7, *Libation* Bearers 1–5, and especially *Eumenides* 1–33.

28 At *Eumenides* 656–66 Apollo claims that Athena's birth is proof that, should he wish, Zeus could do away altogether with women.

requires a progressive reinterpretation of the chthonic—first as ancestors, then as male ancestors (whose names, much as with us, identify the family line), and finally as the elimination of the female.

The *Libation Bearers* is about killing the mother. Motherhood is the one family relationship that seems not mediated. A mother knows immediately that her child is hers. A father can only know by trusting her word. His children are his only by way of *logos*. This is connected to the issue that has dominated our interpretation thus far—the problem of the relation between deed and word, or the problem of interpretation. The meaning of what at first seems immediate, on further reflection proves mediated. Motherhood seems the exception. And yet when Orestes returns, having been sent away by his mother, she does not recognize him. The directness of the maternal connection is a powerful illusion. The mother stands for something important, but she is not that something. What then does she stand for? Mother-killing leads Orestes to go mad. He is pursued by inner furies. He is profoundly at odds with himself. To kill what the mother stands for is to kill what makes oneself possible as a unity; it is what holds one together. So, is the "mother" sanity? And yet, guilt—being at odds with yourself—is born of a deep sense of responsibility, a sense that it is "all your fault." Being at odds with oneself is not so much insanity as sanity heightened, idealized, made pure. It is the sign of a deep inner oneness. In the *Eumenides* Orestes is relieved of this guilt in a way that will make him nothing but a citizen. He will have no mixed loyalties but be the perfect servant of the Olympian gods and feel only what the law tells him to feel. Yet this purified oneness is itself a kind of insanity. The irony of the *Oresteia* is that, by undercutting the "mother," it makes possible perfect citizens—members of a class who are rather like proper nouns than individuals. But in the end, this leads to the complete dissolution of the soul in a kind of madness. And so, in the *Eumenides* it proves necessary for Athena to reintroduce the "mother." Here, in the *Libation Bearers*, Orestes tries to eliminate the mother. This proves to mean that he tries to become completely objective, a perfect self. But a perfect self is not a self at all; its perfection is really a kind of madness. In her attempt to substitute the father for the mother, Electra must disappear. Killing Clytemnestra is not only killing the mother; it is killing the "mother," and this proves to involve more significance than meets the eye.

Logos: *479–782*

Aristotle begins his famous definition of tragedy with the claim that it is "an imitation of action" (*On Poetics* 1449b24), and yet Greek tragedy contains almost no action—nothing like the deeds of *Hamlet*, Act 5. It is all talk—*logos*. Still, one should always take care not to underestimate Aristotle. His definition moves us to wonder what it might mean that the proper imitation of action is *logos*.

While the verb *legein*, to speak, is fairly evenly dispersed throughout the *Libation Bearers*, thirteen of fifteen occurrences of the noun *logos* occur in this section of the play.[29] Why should *logos* be so prominent in the interpretation of Clytemnestra's dream, Orestes' plan to gain entrance to the palace, the chorus' string of mythic examples of women who do evil to their kin, and Orestes' execution of his now revised plan? The answer to this question begins to emerge in the second episode.

The second episode falls into three parts. In the first (479–90), which promises a new burial for Agamemnon, Orestes asks his father for the power of the house, and Electra asks that she may escape after killing Aegisthus. In the second (491–96), they seek to arouse Agamemnon's shame over the manner of his murder. In the third (497–509), there is no mention of burial; mentioning death for the first time, Agamemnon's children declare that they are the only future available to his house, and so to him. The account thus moves from the importance of burial, to the separation of death from burial, to the hope for the future independent

---

29 *Legein* occurs 19 times in the play. While not present in the *parados, kommos*, or the second and third *stasima*, still it occurs at 105, 107, 108, 120, 130, 146, 181, 252, 274, 527, 553, 582, 583, 595, 689, 767, 839, 889, and 1040. *Logos* occurs 15 times (the speaker is indicated in parentheses): 107 (chorus), 509 (Orestes), 510 (chorus), 515 (Orestes), 521 (Orestes), 528 (Orestes), 613 (chorus), 632 (chorus), 659 (Orestes), 666(Orestes), 679 (Orestes), 765 (nurse), 773 (chorus), 781 (nurse), 845 (chorus). These instances display the broad range of meanings *logos* can have—e.g., word, conversation, reason, saying or adage, speech, and news.

of burial. It is a movement away from the chthonic meant to make it possible for Orestes and Electra to treat the dead as dead and not simply as "alive" in another "place." And precisely here the importance of *logos* comes to be emphasized. At 509, Orestes says to his father, "You yourself are preserved in (or: by) this *logos*," and the chorus reply to him "And indeed you are blameless for this extensive *logos*" (presumably because he will make up for it by acting).

There is an additional indication of the centrality of *logos* for this section. Orestes twice uses the poetic plural (480, 491) followed immediately by responses from Electra in the singular (481, 492). The distribution of lines from 500 to 509 is disputed, but line 509 is certainly the last possible speech that Electra gives before she disappears from the play. After she leaves, the chorus seems to replace her as Orestes' coconspirator. And, of course, the chorus are in their peculiar being a perfect example of the poetic plural—twelve people treated as one character. For Orestes it seems important that the particular, the singular, is somehow generic—that he is killing not "mom," but "the mother." Electra, who has actual experiences of living under the particular rule of Clytemnestra and Aegisthus, drops out. It is surely no accident that the atypical prominence of *logos* here should be accompanied by poetic plurals, images of what all *logos* does and must do. Nouns are particulars that are what they are only by virtue of pointing to many things.

Having been urged by the chorus to act immediately, Orestes insists first on learning about Clytemnestra's dream. He wants to know from what *logos* she was moved to send libations to Agamemnon's tomb (515). The *logos* behind his delay would seem to be that he wants to better understand her motives, and so has not yet decided whether to kill her. What leads him to doubt? Granted that the *logos* says libations can never atone for a death (520–21), and therefore Clytemnestra's "gifts are less than her offense" (519), still this need not mean they did not suffice to appease Agamemnon's anger. There is a difference between justice and satisfaction. And since he and Electra did not succeed in summoning their father from the dead, it is necessary to interpret—to give a *logos* to—their failure. This is what it means that Clytemnestra "sent wretched thanks to the unthinking dead" (517). The dead are without thought; accordingly, it is up to the living to somehow interpret what they would have thought.

Orestes' question "From what *logos*" is preceded by "from where (*pothen*) did she send libations" (515). Later (528) he will ask, "where (*poi*) a *logos* may end and be achieved." He uses spatial interrogatives, *pothen* and *poi* ("from where" and "to where"), as though the *logos* of Clytemnestra's motive were something spatial. The chorus answer his question, claiming that they were present and so know that the dream was her reason. It inspired fear. Still, they can only learn of the dream by inquiring. For them, her dream is necessarily a *logos*, for how else could they know it?

Orestes' wish to know about the dream is a way of understanding why Clytemnestra has done what she has done. He wants to understand her action by way of a *logos* and thereby come to know whether her action is likely to have appeased Agamemnon. He wants to know this, in turn, so that he will know whether to kill her. But when Orestes hears the report of the dream he offers an alternative interpretation of it—an interpretation that has nothing whatsoever to do with Clytemnestra's intention. So, sending the libations (an action) gets interpreted (given a *logos*) by seeing how someone reacted to a dream, a dream made public in a *logos* that describes an action. Clytemnestra dreams that having given birth to a snake, when she suckles it, it drinks her blood. When Orestes hears the details of this dream, the action of its plot, he rejects his mother's interpretation—that the snake is Agamemnon, substituting another *logos* in which he is the snake. This *logos* is now taken to be the dream's meaning independent of Clytemnestra's reaction. So, what we would call a symbolic representation gets treated literally, and then reinterpreted independent of the person for whom it was a representation. And this reinterpretation seems to quell Orestes' doubts. That is, what seemed to begin as a question about what Clytemnestra was doing that could be revealed only by how she interpreted her dream becomes a question of what the dream means simply.[30] The consequence of this change is decisive for

---

30 This problem shows up in another way. The chorus report that Clytemnestra said she "anchored it in swaddling clothes like (*dikēn*) a child" (529). In Orestes' interpretation the simile becomes real—he is her child. Oddly, this is suggested by an alternative reading of the passage—that she anchored

the play, for Orestes here for the first time indicates that he will kill his mother (550).[31]

Orestes now announces his plan to gain entrance to the palace. Electra is to go inside (554), although there is no indication that she has a part to play in the enterprise. He will go to the gates (*pulas*) with Pylades (*Puladē$_i$*) (561–62), and pretend to be allies, spear-friends, of the house. The pair will imitate a Phocian dialect (564)—this of course should not prove too difficult since Pylades is in fact Phocian and Orestes has spent his exile in Phocia. Then they will simply wait outside the gates until people start commenting on—giving a *logos* to—their presence. It will be said that there is a supplicant (569), a stranger (*xenos*, 575), at the gates who under the law of guest-friendship (*xenia*) would deserve entry. The plan is to kill Aegisthus either when he comes to the door to ask where they are from or on his throne should he send for them. The plan, however admirable in its simplicity, is fraught with difficulties. Aegisthus, of course, does not come to the door to ask them where they are from (574), and the slave who does come, defying both real and dramatic convention, does not even open the door before asking the question (657). And what about Clytemnestra? How does Orestes intend to get to her once it is known that he has killed Aegisthus? Could this "plan" in fact be designed to prevent that from happening? And why does Orestes assume Aegisthus will come alone? Clytemnestra will send the nurse to summon him and his spearmen (769). It is only because the chorus tell the nurse to suppress the part of the message about the spearmen that Orestes will succeed. The plan, then, is strangely inept. In addition, given that the very events that brought Orestes to this pass, the Trojan War and all its consequences, began with a violation of the law of guest-friendship, the plan is questionable on moral grounds. While Orestes surely has a goal in mind, at the very least the killing of

---

   dikē as justice or punishment in the swaddling clothes of a child. The force of the first version is her behavior as a maker of similes; the force the second version is justice as a reality.
31 Orestes refers to his mother with the pronoun *nin* (550)—which can be masculine, feminine, or neuter. This word will prove very important in the last episode (973–1076).

Aegisthus, he seems to be at a loss as to how to accomplish this goal. He knows what he wishes to accomplish in the house, but he has not thought through what will get him through the door. Orestes has a treatment to sell, but when it comes to producing the details of the script, he proves a singularly incompetent playwright.

We have two issues: the relation between *logos* and action and Orestes' ineptness with respect to plotting. Their connection begins to become clearer in the first stasimon (585–651). The stasimon consists of four strophic pairs. The first (585–601) introduces the category of the *deinos*. It is a strange word. It means both canny and uncanny, clever and terrifying, awesome and awful. The strophe begins with the elements—earth, air, fire, and water—albeit each in some way personified. They are "on the one hand" *deinos*. "But" (*alla*), these are used in the antistrophe as a foil to show there is nothing quite so *deinos* as human beings.[32] In men, the source of the *deinos* is thought—*phronēma* (594); in women it is sexual love—*erōs* (600). And what destroys the pairings of man and woman is the "unloving love" (*aperōtos erōs*, 599–600) of women. The first strophic system means to set the stage for, and to justify, avenging Agamemnon by killing Clytemnestra. The chorus sing this song while Orestes is offstage thinking through his plan to kill his mother. Does the simultaneity of these two suggest the stasimon is meant to indicate the content of Orestes' thinking? Is this what lies behind the sequel—a series of mythic crimes originating in female eros?

The examples of the second strophic system (603–22) prove extremely problematic. In the strophe (603–11), the story of Alythaea is presented as exemplary. She is the mother of the hero Meleager, the man fated to live only as long as a brand burning on the fire at the time of his birth. Alythaea keeps the brand safe until Meleager kills her two brothers, at which point she throws it in the fire, and Meleager perishes. Now the strophe does not contain her name—she is only "the fire-destroying wretched one of Thestius" (605–06). She is described adjectivally and as the offspring of her father. She does not deserve a name. Also, the

---

32   The exemplary character of the human as *deinos* is also the subject of the second stasimon of Sophocles' *Antigone* (332–83), which begins, "Many are the *deinos* things, but none comes more *deinos* than a human being."

story is particularly ill-suited as an exemplar given the chorus's previous claim about the behavior of women. Nowhere does erotic love, unloving or otherwise, play a role. Perhaps most important, the chorus recite the events of the story but without any causal sequence. There is no account whatsoever of how or why Meleager kills his uncles. The antistrophe (612–21) is similar in this regard. Scylla, never named, kills her father, Nisus—perhaps out of eros for Minos (or perhaps she was bribed). This might be similar to what Clytemnestra does if we assume her motive for killing Agamemnon was love for Aegisthus. However, the chorus omit altogether why Minos seeks the help of Scylla. He makes war against Nisus to avenge the death of a child. In this way his motive is not so different from the most compelling of the motives of Clytemnestra. So, the two examples meant to provide a precedent for the crime of Clytemnestra prove curiously inappropriate. As soon as one considers the details the analogies collapse.

Still, the chorus use them to set the stage for the third strophic system (623–38). The strophe (623–30) gives us what we have been awaiting—the story of Clytemnestra—but it is curiously abridged. With the previous two examples as a model, the chorus do not name the villain of their story, omit any mention of Iphigenia, and once again provide no plot details. To be sure, the marriage is "void of love" (*dusphiles*) and "to be prayed away" (*apeucheton*) by the house, the husband is a spear-carrying man, and the scene is a "passionless hearth." Still, absent these modifiers indicating the chorus's view of the action, we are presented with a rather thin plot line: "Wife kills husband."

As a paradigm for understanding the House of Atreus, the antistrophe introduces the Lemnian evil—the oldest in *logos* (631–32). The reference is ambiguous, for the tradition speaks of at least two archetypical evils perpetrated on the island of Lemnos. The story of the first is that the husbands of the women of Lemnos abandon them and take up with slave women. Resenting their abandonment, the Lemnian women kill all the men on the island.[33] Herodotus gives an account of a different

---

33 The fullest extant account of the story is from the *Argonautica* (1. 609–39) of Apollonius of Rhodes, a 3rd century B.C. poet. According to the version in Apollodorus (*Bibliotheca* 1.9.17) from the 2nd or 3rd century A.D., the

evil (6.138) supposedly occurring at a later time when, having sired children with captive slave women, the Lemnian men, out of fear that these
offspring will claim rule in the next generation, kill them as well as their
mothers. At first glance, the two evils seem to represent the tit for tat
character of justice over time. Yet the two events, however much they
seem to have in common, and however much they do deal with eros, are
not really connected, and so justice is really not served. Do the chorus,
then, unwittingly suggest this is true of the events for which they are
presumably meant to serve as a paradigm—the history of the House of
Atreus?

The third strophic system, like the first two, is obtrusively short on
the details of how the events it relates come to be. Here the chorus attribute pretty much all causality to the gods, but this is for them really
just another way of saying that things happened to happen. This proves
true in the final strophic system (639–51) as well. In the strophe, the
chorus give agency to gods—Dike, right or justice, acting on behalf of
Themis, right understood as divine (641), which then is understood in
terms of Zeus (644–45), and in the antistrophe Orestes is brought to the
door of the palace to exact vengeance by Erinys, fury deified (651).

The stasimon as a whole means first to give precedents for what
Orestes is about to do and then to describe what he is about to do. But
while Erinys may bring Orestes to the gate of the palace, it in no way
accounts for how he gets through the gate. This is made quite clear by
his first lines after they finish singing. "Boy! Boy!" (653) is the sign that
his admission to the house will require something more than his fury—
desiring revenge does not guarantee that one gets it. The stasimon provides only an outline of the story—something like "Son avenges father
by killing mother." But the details of the plot that, for example, will get
Orestes into the house are omitted. The chorus begin by claiming eros
is what causes all the evil in this case, but they never get around to describing how. Instead, they veer away to actions not necessarily committed out of passion. In giving us only the bottom line, they provide a

wives do this because Aphrodite has punished their inattentiveness to her
by giving them a foul smell, and it is the smell that drives their husbands
away.

logos that suits *their* purpose but can only do so by leaving out the plotting. Or, put differently, the meaning of the tragic action doesn't get you in the house.[34]

The chorus want to say transgressions against the divine law, whether male or female, owing to thoughts (*phronemata*) or to passionate love (*eros*), are the essence of the human. Because we are in no way restrained by nature, we are the most *deinos* of creatures and must be reined in. This need for the divine, born of our want of any built-in limit, causes our souls to veil their experiences, which as a consequence come forth as gods—Earth, Air, Fire, Water. But this is very like what Orestes does in his interpretation of Clytemnestra's dream. He replaces her interpretation of what she dreamt with his, thereby treating the dream not as her response to her fear but as an objective indicator of something real. Inserting gods into the story as causes (whether Apollo or Erinys) thus allows for the omission of particular actions born of particular motives and essential to the plot. "A god made me do it," is not really plot detail at all. Still, once introduced, the gods take over the experience and reconfigure its story. When anger or fury gets personified as Erinys, it is no longer my anger that causes me to do what I do.[35]

The gods may be the paradigm for such transformations, but their significance extends beyond the gods. One need only think of the title of this play. Libation bearers is a generic way of describing both Electra and the chorus who accompany her. They all manifest *thrēnos*, mourning. But, as we have seen, Orestes distinguishes between Electra and the chorus on the basis of whether their external *thrēnos* is a sign of

34 Orestes' "Boy! Boy!"—*pai pai*—at 653 recalls *Agamemnon* 1144 where in warning of the death of Agamemnon, Cassandra cries out *papai, papai*. But, of course the words of warning are not enough. The chorus do not understand what she is saying. Words, meanings, are not the same as deeds. Not the heart-rending *papai, papai*, but the dull details, the *pai, pai*, are what actually accomplish things.

35 When Athena pulls Achilles' hair to prevent him from attacking Agamemnon an inner tension gets transformed into an external event. Refraining from killing Agamemnon is no longer an action of Achilles for which he, as agent, is responsible; it is rather something he undergoes. See *Iliad* 1.194–218.

genuine internal grief. To be sure, his discrimination is not altogether successful, for he does not see that, while the chorus do not genuinely mourn for Agamemnon, they do feel inner grief for their own dead. The inner is not so easy to distinguish from its outer sign. The conventional formula for mourning becomes so powerful for us that unless it is performed—unless cheeks are raked and clothing rent—we assume mourning to be inadequate. We assume the mourners do not really care. The *Libation Bearers* means to remind us of all of this. It first shows us Orestes' own understanding of what he is going to do. It then supplements this with an account of how what he means to do would be impossible without certain events of which he never becomes aware. The conversation that begins with his *pai pai* announces the presence of this sort of "insignificant" detail. One must always go through "slaves." This is further fleshed out by the roles taken by the chorus and the nurse, without whom Aegisthus would have returned with his guard, and Orestes' plan would have been foiled. The *Libation Bearers* seems to give us two sorts of *logos*—high and low, tragic and rather comic. It is generally characteristic of comic characters to have a plan, to attend to plotting—we laugh when Don Quixote wants to know where knights keep their spare undergarments, and we never expect King Lear to relieve himself.

The discrepancy between principles and plotting becomes still more evident in what follows. Before the stasimon, Orestes proposes to the chorus that he will enter the palace by way of disguising himself as a military ally—spear-guest-friend (*doruxenos*, 562). During the time when the chorus sing the stasimon, he changes his mind, abandons this plan, and devises another. He will now be a messenger announcing the death of Orestes (682). It is at the very time Orestes is concocting this new story that the chorus discover that they cannot get to their *logos* of the human soul apart from stories. They tell two that are not really appropriate and then tell a third, the story of the Lemnian evil, that they find satisfactory. Then they return to the action at hand, the contemplated matricide of Clytemnestra, for which, surprisingly, none of their stories seems to provide a precedent. Their public difficulty justifying matricide seems meant to show us Orestes' private difficulty settling on a plan. Orestes moves from a story in which he is important—a potential ally—

to a story in which he disappears. He becomes a nobody, an anonymous messenger who brings word of the death of "Orestes."

Orestes' *pai pai* at 652 echoes the language of the comic stage.[36] A slave boy (whom we never see) responds to it from within the house, "Well, I hear. A stranger from what country? From where?" (667).[37] Perhaps Orestes has to change his story and improvise because the slave has asked the question that Orestes expected Aegisthus to ask. He must now claim entrance not simply as a generic ally but as someone with crucial news to impart, news so important that it can only be told to one bearing authority (*telesphoros*, 663)—perhaps the woman of the house, but preferably a man with whom one can speak a *logos* more boldly and with less reverence (664–66). It is apparently a male thing to make evidence clear (666–67). Orestes' ploy is designed to induce the slave to fetch Aegisthus rather than Clytemnestra, but to do so it must affirm a connection between *logos* and the male.

Orestes' plan begins to unravel immediately with what Clytemnestra says as she enters.

> Strangers, would that you say if you need something, for
> whatever sort is fitting for this house is present—both hot
> baths and bedding that charms away toils, and the presence
> of just eyes. But if it is necessary to act on something else,
> something requiring more counsel, this is a deed of men, with
> whom we will share it. (668–73)

Because Orestes will not be taken to Aegisthus immediately, but is to be shown to the men's quarters (to the bath where his father was killed?), he improvises—he must think up something to speak of that requires the presence of the man of the house. Strangely, his story about the death

36 In Aristophanes' *Clouds* (132) the loutish Strepsiades shouts *pai paidion* (little boy) and later (1145) *pai pai* when he seeks to gain entrance to Socrates' school. In the *Acharnians* (395), Dikaiopolis yells *pai, pai* at Euripides' door to ask whether Euripides is in or out.

37 Like Pylades he has only one line in the play, the single case in the extant Greek tragedies of an exchange between a character on stage and one off stage.

of "Orestes" does in a way require his death. He claims to be no one in particular, just someone on the way to Argos (we are not told why) when by accident, "an unknown to an unknown" (677), he met Strophius, Pylades' father, who then asked him to bring news of the death of Orestes to his "parents" (681). This story is peculiar in the strangely haphazard way Strophius chooses deliver news of a death in the family. Orestes might have chosen another story or another course of action. He could have killed Clytemnestra on the spot. Has he yet made the decision to kill her? Is his "improvisation" really meant to reveal how his mother will react to his death? In stark contrast to his former nurse, who will soon utter an extended lamentation (734–65), Clytemnestra has not yet even recognized her son.

Clytemnestra's "lamentation" is peculiarly ambiguous.[38] On the one hand, she claims that Orestes' death completes the process of stripping her bare of friends (695); on the other hand, she says that when she shares the news with the ruler of the house, they will have no scarcity of friends (717). We do not know—perhaps she does not know— whether she is saddened or pleased by the death of her son. The nurse, less ambivalent, describes Clytemnestra as,

> on the one hand, toward the servants putting on a look of sadness, but, on the other hand, eyes laughing within covering over deeds having been accomplished beautifully . . . . (737– 39)

The nurse goes on to present herself as in a way more truly the mother of Orestes than Clytemnestra. Her argument involves appeals to plotting details found on the comic stage. She tended to Orestes' needs as a baby, as an "unthinking thing" (753)—nursing him, changing and washing his swaddling clothes. Since he did not yet have *logos*, to know when he

---

38 She begins with *Oi'gō*—"Ah, me/I" (691). This expression occurs only three times in the play and only in the mouth of Clytemnestra—here, when she learns of the death of Aegisthus (691), and just before she exits with Orestes on the way to her own death (928). The "I" is always present in Clytemnestra's expressions of grief.

was hungry or thirsty, when he needed to piss or shit, required an art of interpretation. Really raising a child means not being able to have everything turn out perfectly; it means dealing with the accidental and unpredictable. Dealing with loose ends is what the chorus and the nurse do to fill out Orestes' plan. Orestes concocts a way to assure *that* Clytemnestra will summon Aegisthus, but never thinks through *how* she will do so. Slaves, "invisible" actors, attend to these details. The chorus and the nurse—who together make sure that Aegisthus will come alone without his guard of armed men—complete the plot of a story that Orestes has provided only in outline.

Human beings are in their origins unthinking. That Orestes and Clytemnestra do not recognize each other, that the nurse can claim to be the "true" mother of Orestes, points to the problem at the heart not only of this cursed family, but of every family. Orestes calls Aegisthus the male parent (*tektonta*—690) of the dead "Orestes." Aegisthus is presumably by law or *nomos* the father of Orestes now that Agamemnon is dead. But are not all fathers somehow fathers by *nomos*, fathers because of the roles they enact in word—in a story, a plot, a *muthos*? Fatherhood is always a matter of interpretation—of *logos*. It can be known only mediately by way of the word, the *muthos*, the *logos*, of the mother. The family presents itself as the non-mediated, non-abstract connection. In this light, it seems our surest and deepest connection. But, in fact, it is a *muthos* without plotting, and one for which it is in principle impossible to provide an adequate plot. To be born means to be an "unthinking thing"—to be in a story for which one can never provide the details.[39] At first it seems that only mothers are in possession of these plotting details—only mothers have an immediate relation to their children and know them as more than legitimately their own. But Aeschylus deprives Clytemnestra of this certainty by having her send Orestes away as a child. She does not recognize him when he returns. Once the chain of evidence is broken, Clytemnestra is in the situation all non-mothers are in. In a way, the mother has already been killed.

The first stasimon is somehow the key to this problem. We saw that in trying to articulate the horror of killing kin, the chorus mean to provide

---

39 Think of how children are prone to wonder if they have been adopted.

examples that disclose the sacredness of the family bond. But that they leave out all the details serves as a sign that the crucial details can never be filled in. There is something necessarily mythic about the power of the family. The emblem of this mythic power is the mother. The problem of the *Libation Bearers* is in a way simple. It is a play about mother-killing because it attempts to reveal the truth about motherhood by deconstructing motherhood—the strongest possible candidate for a self-evident and immediate link between human beings. It means to reveal the longing for such a self-evident link and to deny the possibility of its full realization. Still, what does this have to do with the "obvious" theme of the play and indeed of the trilogy as a whole, i.e., justice?

The Deaths of Clytemnestra and Aegisthus: 783–930

In the second stasimon (783–837) the chorus pray for the success of Orestes. It is followed by the death of Aegisthus (838–80) and the death of Clytemnestra (881–930). The text of the stasimon is unusually corrupt, frequently amounting to little more than headings that show us what is at issue but are not put together into sentences.[40] It divides into three strophic systems—each with a strophe, mesode, and antistrophe. Roughly, the theme of first system is the moderating of Orestes; of the second, the relation among three different sorts of gods—the ancestral, Apollo, and Hermes; and of the third, advice to Orestes about how to confront Clytemnestra. This last is rather peculiar since Orestes is not present, and the chorus seem to think he is at this moment in the house killing his mother. They think they have arranged things so that Orestes can kill his mother behind closed doors without revealing who he is, and so that thereafter Aegisthus will arrive unarmed and be killed. But Orestes does not do what the chorus "tell" him to do. He reverses the order of the deaths and, after killing Aegisthus, confronts Clytemnestra openly.

In the first strophic system (783–99), the chorus pray to Zeus, but the corruption of the text makes it impossible to know who or what they

---

40 It differs from the first stasimon in its use of proper names—Zeus (784, 790), Maia (813) and Perseus (831).

are praying for. The strophe (783–88) is particularly difficult to make out. Still, the concluding line, *Zeu, su nin phulassois* (788), at first seems clear enough—"Zeus, would that you watch over him." However, *nin* may be translated "him," "her," or "it." Is its antecedent the feminine *dikas*, justice (787), or is it the feminine *tuchas*, fortune (785)? Or is it Orestes? Is it something neuter that has dropped from our text? The text is corrupt, to be sure, but even were it sound, the meaning of *nin* would be ambiguous. As far as one can tell, the theme of the strophe is moderation; it is a prayer to Zeus to keep Orestes on an even keel, sane, so that he can accomplish his purpose. The mesode (789–93) does not seem to introduce much that is new, but once again we find an ambiguous *nin* (791). What do they mean to urge Zeus to raise to greatness—Orestes or his house? In the antistrophe (794–99), they liken Orestes to a colt and call upon Zeus to make his running *metron*, measured, so as to have a rhythm (797). On the one hand, this seems merely another call to moderation. On the other hand, both the metaphor itself and the language it uses, meter and rhythm, suggest that this sanity they request has something to do with poetry.

In the second strophic system (800–18), the strophe (800–06) addresses those within the innermost chamber of the house. It is a call to the ancestral gods of the hearth for the taking of new blood in a new act of justice for an old murder. It is an appeal to the gods of the past to avenge past wrongs. The mesode (807–11) is an appeal to another god, Apollo, in another inner chamber, the cave beneath his temple at Delphi where his oracles originated. They appeal to the god of prophecy and light to bring freedom. But freedom of whom or of what? Once again, we find an ambiguous *nin*. Do they pray for the freedom of the man, presumably Orestes, or for the house of the man? Whatever may be the case, the mesode is an appeal to a new god and concerns the future. The antistrophe (812–18) is an appeal to Hermes (who we remember was addressed in the first word of the play) to contribute by way of stealth to Orestes' success. As Orestes is at this very moment within the house, the antistrophe is an appeal to the go-between god about the present. Accordingly, in the second strophic system, albeit for reasons not immediately clear, the issue is time—past, future, present.

It is in the third strophic system (819–37) that the chorus give their own advice to the absent Orestes about how to confront Clytemnestra. The strophe (819–26) makes clear that they are not simply neutral observers to this drama; they have an interest. They anticipate "release from the house" (820) and will sing the song (*nomon*, which also means "law"—824), "these things sail well; this augments my gain, and destruction stands far from those loved" (824–26). The killing of Clytemnestra will redound to their benefit. It is apparently their freedom that was at issue in the second mesode.

The mesode of the third system (827–31) is at once initially unclear and especially revealing.

> And you, being bold, when you have come to work out your part,
> shouting the sound of "father"
> to her who cries aloud "child,"
> accomplish a blameless ruin.

The chorus imagine Clytemnestra saying, "You are the child," and, if the structure of their sentence is parallel, as one would expect it to be, Orestes would reply "No, I am the father." In the real conversation that follows between Orestes and Clytemnestra (907–09), when she offers to live and grow old with him, Orestes replies, "You would co-habit with me, being a father killer?" Agamemnon may have been his father, but he is not father to Clytemnestra. She did not commit patricide. Later (1005–006) Orestes will say, "Would that such a co-habiter not come to be in my house; sooner would I perish, childless from the gods!" He thus imagines Clytemnestra to live with him as though she were his spouse, not his mother. Orestes must *be* the father to justify what he is about to do. The chorus seem to think Orestes will achieve blamelessness by not acknowledging Clytemnestra as his mother. Taking on the role of father reminds us of the earlier failed attempt to call Agamemnon back from the dead.[41] The "natural" way to read the mesode (and the

---

41 Could there be yet a different interpretation of the chorus's imagined exchange? Clytemnestra would say "child," and mean "Iphigenia"; Orestes would say "father," and mean "Agamemnon." In this way, neither would be affirming a relation to the other, and justice might be served.

way many translators read the passage), i.e., what we think it ought to mean, seems to be for Clytemnestra to say, "You are my son," and Orestes to reply, "but what about my father?"[42] But this is only really possible if there is no parallel structure in the sentence. The illusion of parallel structure—she shouts "child"; he shouts "father"—is necessary if the chorus is to hold Orestes blameless, and the killing just. Yet it is an illusion—Orestes' response to Clytemnestra cannot be like Clytemnestra's response to Orestes. The structure may suggest it is "tit for tat," but "tit" is not "tat."

The problem of the mesode points to the third antistrophe (832–37) where the chorus advise Orestes to have the heart of Perseus (832–33). They imply that he should kill Clytemnestra, as Perseus killed the Gorgon, without looking at her. The problem is that this advice is given when Orestes cannot hear it. Had he heard and taken it, he would have killed her during the stasimon with no confrontation with the mother, or at least with no confrontation visible to us. The chorus do not say to Orestes "Act like Perseus!" Instead, they urge him to have the heart of Perseus in his breast. They translate Perseus's action into an attitude of soul that is really not possible. It is as though they were to tell him, "Do not think about what I am saying; just do it." Or, "Do not look at the mother, and so feel no shame in what you are about to do." But this is the problem that has haunted Orestes from the beginning of the play. The chorus utter their advice when he is not present because to utter it at all is to undermine it. They cannot tell him "Don't think about your mother" without causing him to think about his mother. That Orestes has been brooding on this is clear from the fact that he does not utter the word "mother" until just before killing Clytemnestra, where he connects it with shame (899).

The second stasimon begins with the chorus asking Zeus to give Orestes moderation—*sōphrosunē*. It ends with his shame—*aidōs*—before the mother. Both are designed to prevent extremism, craziness—to keep one sane. Moderation, however, seems designed to replace shame as the human awareness that there is a limit on the human. We come to

42 See, for example, *Aeschylus: The Oresteia*, Hugh Lloyd-Jones trans. (Berkeley: University of California Press, 1979), 178.

know there are certain things we cannot do and still remain who we are. In this way, we know our identities by way of our knowledge of our limitations. Adam and Eve cover themselves in shame as they emerge from Eden and discover that they are man and woman—each only partially human. As shame, this knowledge of our limits is also a limit on the power that the gods have over us. It is the sign that there is something we as ourselves cannot do—something that has nothing to do with the commands of a god. But when shame is replaced by moderation, what previously came from within is now understood to come from without—from the gods. Inexplicable shame becomes intelligible obedience. Thus, in the second strophic system we are presented with past, future, and present, but in the third strophic system, the past (and with it, the gods peculiar to me—my ancestors) drops out. It is the past that announces the power of what was, simply because it was—a power of what happens to be, what must be now but need not have been, and a power of unknown meaning not grounded in an articulable universal principle. This bondage to the past is akin to our attachment to our mothers, our families, and our ancestors.[43]

How then does the replacement of shame by moderation work? To rid ourselves of the shame that attaches to particularity we make it public. We turn private motives into "Apollo told me to do it." Or, "I do what is lawful and only what is lawful." We transform shame into a virtue, moderation—something we do because it is beautiful or noble, and so for its own sake and not out of shame. In the first antistrophe of the second stasimon, the chorus make Orestes a colt and call upon Zeus to give him meter and rhythm. And in the third strophe they understand their own future as singing a *nomos*, a song or a law, that their "ship goes well."

Now this movement parallels the movement of the whole trilogy and especially the movement from the *Libation Bearers* to the *Eumenides*. Orestes cannot avoid confronting his mother as mother. Therefore, he feels shame even as he kills her. He cannot obey Apollo and kill her in stealth; he cannot preserve his anonymity, his detachment from

---

43 This underlies Aristotle's claim at *On Poetics* 1451b6 that poetry is more philosophic than history.

her. But in killing Clytemnestra as mother, he gives her new life. He goes mad with guilt.[44] Orestes exits the *Libation Bearers* pursued by inner furies seen by him but by no one else. Aeschylus follows this action with the final play, the *Eumenides*, in which a representation of Orestes' madness—of the inner, particular principle, the mother principle—is put on a par with the Olympian gods. The Furies are externalized and visible to all. These Furies engage in a contest with Apollo over Orestes, but it is a contest they have already lost, and necessarily so. Their core, their internality, has been sacrificed by being represented and made external. When we see them as representation of madness, the old gods are transformed, but once they are out of the soul it is impossible to put them back in. By being represented, the inner has been tamed. The Furies become *eu-menides*, good or kindly anger.[45] This transformation is in a way implicit in all political life. Politics attempts to make the human being, who is *deinos*/uncanny/terrible/unpredictable into a citizen who is *deinos*/canny/clever/predictable. This would mean the total victory of the Olympian principle (in the *Eumenides*, Apollo claims that Zeus could do away with the female altogether, 657–66) and with it the total destruction of the human. Accordingly, Clytemnestra represents the greatest threat to the Olympian gods. Of the three killings featured in the *Oresteia* (of Iphigenia, of Agamemnon, and of Clytemnestra), only her killing of Agamemnon proceeds by way of a solely human motive with no divine intervention. Her gut tells her to kill him, not a representation of her gut. This, in turn, is connected to the fact that in Orestes' report of the oracle, only the two lines (276–77) having to do with Orestes' soul are in direct discourse. And there is no explicit content to the ills the lines threaten for Orestes' soul. His inner suffering cannot be brought into speech without being tamed.

Orestes kills Aegisthus before he kills Clytemnestra. Aegisthus comes home because a messenger (presumably the nurse) summoned him with a new *phatis* of Orestes' lot; *phatis* has many meanings—for

---

44   In the *Eumenides* (94–39), Clytemnestra will haunt the Furies who haunt Orestes.

45   See Benardete, "The Furies of Aeschylus" (65) and "On Greek Tragedy" (123), both in *The Argument of the Action*.

example, "word," "rumor," or "oracle"—and so the status of the news brought to Aegisthus is unclear. The chorus's subsequent remark about the unreliability of messengers (the plural is interesting, 849) underlines this unclarity. They encourage Aegisthus's preference for questioning the strangers himself. Pushed to its logical conclusion his mistrust would extend to a mistrust of any report whatsoever as mediated, and so, in principle, would be a mistrust of all *logos*. Aegisthus is suspicious of the news: "How am I to suppose (*doxasō*—also, imagine or opine) these things true and seen?" Aegisthus wants to *see* the messenger (singular) to learn how he knows. Is it by hearsay—i.e., by "knowledge" already mediated through others—or by being himself present at Orestes' death? Aegisthus knows that *logos* is only reliable when it is somehow tied down to a particular reality. He wants to see and question the messenger because in his manly way, he believes that "a mind having open eyes cannot be deceived" (854). Aegisthus has thus unwittingly brought into play the problem of authentic knowledge. How is it possible to put together the universal, mind, the common noun, and the Olympians as principles (e.g., Ares as war)—i.e., what seems necessarily mediated, with the particular, sight, proper nouns, ancestors, and the chthonic gods—i.e., with the mother "principle," what seems necessarily immediate?

The chorus sing as Aegisthus, having entered the house, is being killed (855–67). Wishing to invoke the gods, they do not know what to say (855). They have "good will" (literally, "good mind"), but how are they to speak equitably (857–58) in the name of lighting "a fire for freedom" (863)? But whose freedom? Coming directly after Aegisthus's remarks about the untrustworthiness of *logos*, their *logos* calls attention to its own ambiguities. Their mind may be good, but their intent is and remains unknown. Their incomplete partisanship is clear when they later say they plan to stand aside so that however things turn out, they will seem blameless (872–73).

In the *Agamemnon*, the killing of Iphigenia is presented as having been motivated by the gods (Agamemnon had no particular desire for her death), while Clytemnestra has a solely human motive for killing Agamemnon. The gods do not move her. In the *Libation Bearers*, Orestes is motivated in both ways, but the human motivation is putatively replaced by the divine. This is really the plot of the play. In the

Eumenides, all the motivation is from the gods, but the gods now come in two types—the Olympians and the Furies—chthonic gods who are external representations of human motives. The *Eumenides* is an account of the founding of the Athenian jury system; it resolves the tension between divine and human motivation in the political life. This tension in the *Oresteia* between the human and the divine, and its "resolution" in the political, is the tension within *logos* writ large. It is the apparent victory of the male, the continuing and necessary power of the female. Only Clytemnestra appears in all three plays of the *Oresteia*, and she is by far the most impressive character of the trilogy.

When she encounters the corpse of Aegisthus, Clytemnestra's first thought is to lament his death saying that she has understood the word of the servant couched in riddles (887). This will have the effect of making her confrontation with Orestes turn on his charge of adultery rather than, for example, on her avenging Iphigenia. It will be shaky ground for her. Her second thought is to acknowledge that they will suffer in turn what they have meted out—that having destroyed Agamemnon by guile, they will be killed similarly (888). She expects no special treatment. Her third, scarcely the stereotypical "woman's" response, is to call for a man-slaying axe so that she can seek victory in battle (889).

There are additional curiosities in their exchange. Threatened by Orestes, Clytemnestra says, "Hold, son, and be shamed by what is before you, child!" (896). Orestes would feel *aidōs* before the mother but not before the adulteress. Clytemnestra calls him son and child, and yet Orestes has not announced who he is. What does it mean that she suddenly recognizes him? Or does the fact that she told Aegisthus to come accompanied by guards (769) mean that from the very beginning she suspected that the stranger was Orestes? At 899–902, Pylades utters his sole speech of the play. It is a response to Orestes' first use of the word "mother": "Pylades, what am I to do? Should I be ashamed to kill a mother?" (900). The otherwise voiceless character then urges Orestes to replace this internal shame with trust in the oracles of Apollo. The man who never speaks does say one thing: Obey the gods! In a world where we accept this, would there be any point to *logos*? Orestes several times (e.g., at 974) calls Clytemnestra father-killer. He never sees the situation from her side—i.e., she is a husband-killer not a father-killer. And when he says he will never cohabit with Clytemnestra (908), and so treats her as a potential spouse, he takes on the identity of Agamemnon. In unwittingly assuming his particular perspective to be a universal perspective, Orestes does what we are all in some way guilty of. And why does Clytemnestra never mention Iphigenia? In having her come close to doing so ("Speak similarly of the follies of your father."—918), Aeschylus merely calls attention to the fact that she does not do so. By not mentioning Iphigenia, Clytemnestra allows Orestes to assume he was sent away to facilitate her adultery with Aegisthus (917).

Orestes kills Clytemnestra during the third stasimon (931–72). The stasimon begins with a short introduction (931–34), followed by two strophic systems (935–52 and 953–72), each consisting of a strophe, mesode, and antistrophe. The chorus begin by saying they "groan for a double misfortune of these" (931). Do they suggest there are two sides of the story—that of Orestes and that of Clytemnestra? Even so, they side with Orestes. Why? To preserve the house. The house, then, is the male house. This seems connected to the singular "house of Agamemnon" at 937—here, the house is not its customary poetic plural. They now speak of the house as completely purged of its doubleness—of its combination of maleness and femaleness. This, in turn, is connected to the series of male gods mentioned here.[46] And this, the male, is the eye of the house—the part that sees (934).

The first strophe (935–41) begins with a deep ambiguity. It seems at first to say that, although it took time, the sons of Priam were punished for the unjust abduction of Helen. But it could just as easily mean that justice came on behalf of the sons of Priam—that it took time, but Orestes is unwittingly about to avenge them and free these Trojan slaves. Orestes would then, as an instrument who does not exercise his own will, be a subject who is also an object. This, in turn, is connected to the dualisms that follow. Orestes is twice a lion and twice Ares, god of war, because his one deed avenges in a double way. The ambiguity is continued in the mesode, where the chorus call for shouting out in joy for the escape of the

---

46 Ares (938), Apollo (940 and 952), and Zeus (949). It is connected as well to the conventional practice among us, only recently called into question, of adopting the name of the husband as the family surname.

houses of the masters from evils and the wasting of wealth by a polluted pair (943–44). As usual, of course, "houses" could be a poetic plural and mean "house," or for that matter, since *domos* may also mean "room," its plural "rooms" may mean "house" as a collection of rooms. Still, if *domōn* were an ordinary genitive plural, it could mean "of the houses," and so point to the houses of both Agamemnon and Priam. The same ambiguity holds for the polluted pair at 944, which may mean the pair of households, one in Argos and one in Troy. It is not so easy to escape the particular by way of the general—to escape shame by way of moderation.

In the antistrophe (946–51), the chorus hail the coming of one who will bring retribution by stealth, one whose hand is guided by a "true daughter of Zeus, Justice." In Greek this reads *etētumos Dios kora, Dikan*. So, we are given an etymological argument (notice the word for true—*etētumos*). *Dios kora* (daughter of Zeus), by elision becomes *Dika* (Justice). An etymology poses as a genealogy. Generation by way of a particular mother and father is replaced by a generation totally in *logos*—totally male. This is a prefiguring of what it means for Athena to be born full grown from the head of Zeus, her "mother" said to be *mētis* (either "mind" or "no one"). Now, generation without procreation is like coming to be without plotting, with just meaning—as though to generate a human being one somehow puts "rational" and "animal" together in a pot and stirs. In time, of course, *Dikē* can come to be only by way of plotting—in this case, for example, by way of an instrument like Orestes who, rather like a slave, does not really know what he is doing, and therefore whose motives cannot be simply just. On the level of plotting, *Dios kora* would mean not Athena, but Helen, daughter of Leda and Zeus disguised as a swan, Helen, the cause of the Trojan War who had no intention of causing the Trojan War. The chorus's affirmation of justice in time in the first antistrophe, therefore, seems to have an undercurrent of justice as of necessity imperfect owing to the necessity of plotting by way of beings who are never simply empty vessels to be used, each having individual axes to grind. Human beings are always both agents and patients and so never simply either. They are not like gods, who are at once pure patients or meanings—e.g., Ares as war— and pure agents or wills—e.g., Ares as the person who sleeps with Aphrodite. Like the chorus, human beings are slaves who seek freedom.

The strophe (953–60) of the second strophic system (953–72) cites as worthy of reverence the "rule of heaven" (960) as punishing evil, even if this punishment is sometimes delayed over time (955), and cites Apollo's oracles as proof that the gods eventually prevail. However, the delay of justice seems owing to the notorious ambiguity of these oracles, what is here called Apollo's "guileless guile" (955), and is imitated by the ambiguity of the end of the sentence; the verb *epoichetai* may mean either that Apollo attacks the ancient harm to men or that he visits harm upon them. But this is just the character of acts of justice that unfold in time, where the righting of a past wrong is necessarily imperfect and so must simultaneously enact a present wrong that will call for being righted in the future. This difficulty shows up as well in the mesode (962–65) when the chorus address the house—presumably of Atreus (if *oikōn*, houses, is a poetic plural) or houses—presumably of Atreus and of Priam (if it is an ordinary plural). The House of Atreus is like the New York Yankees. What does it actually mean to say a team has won 27 World Series Championships? Why is the team with Lou Gehrig at first base the same as the team with Bill Skowron or Tino Martinez at first base? If over time justice is finally meted out to the House of Atreus, what good does that do Thyestes, who was tricked into eating his own children? Justice "over time" is never justice as experienced by an individual—even if the time is one's own lifetime. If one is wrongly imprisoned, that the mistake is later realized does not undo the harm done. The second antistrophe (965–72) deals directly with this problem. From one point of view, one suffers a wrong—Clytemnestra by Agamemnon, Agamemnon by Clytemnestra, Orestes by Clytemnestra, Clytemnestra by Orestes. From another point of view, a wrong is righted. This seems the necessary consequence of visiting divine justice by way of the actions of men in time. It is the problem of mixing together universal meaning with particular events. It is the problem of *logos* to which the last episode of the play returns.

The Aftermath: 973–1076

Having killed Clytemnestra and Aegisthus, Orestes wishes to defend his action—to display their guilt. He has killed the conventional father and the natural mother, and in restoring his "house," he has sought to restore the unity of the family. He begins with a long speech in which many editors have been tempted to think the pieces are out of order. Accordingly, they reorder the text to avoid difficulties.[47] But it is the business of poetry to unsettle us with difficulties—to startle us with the unconventional use of *logos*. Poets write metaphorically in order to stir us from dogmatic slumber by revealing to us the strangeness of the ordinary. What then might the strangeness of Orestes' speech be meant to bring into the open?

Orestes begins by displaying the corpses of Aegisthus and Clytemnestra, calling them the "double tyranny" (973) of the land. However, that they are a double tyranny cannot be self-evident from their dead bodies, or else Orestes would not have to go on to explain his action. He must provide a justification for his action—a *logos* of some kind. Accordingly, he points to the net-like covering, the cloth or cloak, that was used to restrain Agamemnon in his bath prior to killing him. Orestes first calls it a device (*mēchanēma* 981), which he glosses as shackles (*pedas*) for a pair of hands and a pair of fetters (*xunorida*) for a pair of feet (983); then a trap (*agreuma* 998); a covering or drape (*kataskēnōma* 999) over the feet of a corpse; a net (*diktuon* 999); a hunting net (*arkun* 1000); and foot-entangling robes (*peplous* 1000). Now, if Orestes must use so many words to describe this object, is its meaning so much more self-evident than the bodies it is meant to shed light on?

The problem of self-evident meaning emerges in the text that editors want to move because of the abruptness of its transition from Clytemnestra to whatever we are to call the net. Orestes seems to finish with Clytemnestra at 996 when he says, "for the sake of the daring of an evilly unjust purpose," and then move very abruptly to "it"—i.e., the net—at 997. But this abruptness, and the gap of meaning it induces, is really just the point. Orestes starts by comparing Clytemnestra to a snake (994). Then he says:

47 Sensing this difficulty, Lloyd Jones reorders the text, justifying it as follows: "The transposition adopted in the text [moving lines 997–1004 so that they follow line 990] was suggested only during the present century [the 20th], but it removes more than one serious difficulty better than any other suggested expedients."

ti nin prōseipō; ("In what way shall I address her/it?"). As we saw earlier, *nin* is a third person singular pronoun that may mean him, her, or it. Since Orestes has just been speaking about Clytemnestra, the most natural way to take *nin* would be "her." But in what follows it is clear that he has made the transition from talking about her to talking about the net. The ambiguity of meaning here is wonderfully revealing for the speech because, by itself, it points to the problem of the speech. Orestes means to say, "I will show you Clytemnestra's guilt," but this must mean, "I will show you her soul." Without exposing her motive, what lies within, her guilt will not become manifest. It is at this point where he points to the net and says, "Look at it/her." The problem, though, is that by itself, the net is mute— it says nothing. There is an unbridgeable gap between "her" and "it" that *nin* artfully finesses. The net needs an interpretation. And this is precisely what Orestes proceeds to give it. It is, he tells us, the sort of thing used by a knavish man to cheat strangers living the life of a robber and killing many by guile (1001–004). The account at first seems a plausible description until you realize that what you have in front of you is just a piece of cloth, difficult to name because it has a variety of possible functions. To be sure it is bloody, but the blood might just as easily have come from trying to stanch a wound as from the murder of Agamemnon. Orestes wants to give the cloth meaning, but he has been working backwards from the meaning he wants it to have.

Of course, we have seen this sort of thing before. By themselves, the locks of Orestes' hair with which the *Libation Bearers* begins, the leprosy he imagines to be punishment, and the bloody net are meaningless. They have meaning only when embedded in a sequence of events, a plot or *muthos*. It is perhaps more correct to say that we try to give them meaning by so embedding them. In this way, they become representations of what we can never get at in itself—soul. Orestes has a need to display Clytemnestra's soul to the chorus so that they can see her guilt, but all they really get here is a bloody cloth. To make the cloth significant, Orestes must re-embed it in another story—the poetic story about the robber. But, of course, his original purpose was to make sense of events in a story, the death of Agamemnon, by appealing to the cloth.

The underlying meaning of the speech, then? Things are significant only insofar as they are things for a soul. Accordingly, to get at the significance of things requires getting at the soul for whom they are significant. It is not leprosy but Orestes' interpretation of leprosy that constitutes his punishment. We have seen that meting out justice is impossible without getting inside the soul—without understanding motive. The rub is that where stories are necessary to give things meaning, a real story involves real particular details, and these real details which, in turn, always involve multiple possible *aitiai*—causes or blame. Why did Clytemnestra kill Agamemnon? Revenge for the sacrifice of Iphigenia? A desire to continue ruling in Argos? Her wish to replace him with Aegisthus? That Agamemnon intends to introduce Cassandra into their household? Any of these, or any combination of them, would suffice as a motive. How could Orestes know for certain? Indeed, how could even Clytemnestra know for certain why she does what she does? The particularity of any real soul guarantees that it has a certain opacity. If it is to be soul at all, soul must retain some measure of unpredictability. Still, however problematic, our need to assign motive requires that we penetrate this opacity. Embedding things in stories is our access to soul. This is what occurs in a jury trial. We seek to understand the correct story, one that adequately puts the details together into an intelligible whole. And yet the details of stories always give us a superfluity, and so necessarily undermine the meaning we seek. A jury trial aims at certainty. This would require a story that is at once particular (and so real) and universal (and so intelligible). Such a story would be exemplary or paradigmatic—poetic.[48] *Logos* is always poetic insofar as in pointing to the world, it must point as well to its own limits.

In the *Libation Bearers*, the tension between universal and particular surfaces in the way Orestes' "plan" proves inadequate. His inadequacy at first appears comic. When Orestes utters his comic cry "Boy! Boy!", it does not achieve the anticipated result. Having a soul, the boy proves unpredictable, and Orestes must ad lib to gain entrance to the palace. The nurse is unpredictably so devoted to Orestes that she disobeys his mother and does not tell Aegisthus to come attended by guards. This

---

48 This seems to be why Aeschylus calls attention to the meaning of *dikēn* (normally the accusative of "justice") as "like" or "just as" to introduce similes. Justice is always poetic justice. See note 20 above.

devotion shows up comically in her speech about changing his diapers—that is, in a story that belongs to the comic stage. The speech suggests a distinction between Clytemnestra as *the* mother, mother in principle, mother as such, mother as noun, and the nurse as Orestes' actual, particular mother. Finally, Orestes' plan would have failed without the intervention of the chorus, who see that they must convince the nurse to alter Clytemnestra's request to Aegisthus. But the motive for, and therefore the extent of, the loyalty of the chorus is never altogether clear. They might easily have acted otherwise. The nurse, the boy, the chorus, who know they are slaves, are not translatable into nouns, principles. They are individuals.

What is at stake here is a tension between the male principle, meaning as such without particulars, the father, what is fully in the open and intelligible, the Olympian gods, knowledge as mediated, the city and *nomos*—namely, what it is possible to put into *logos*; and the female principle, particularity, the family, the mother, the chthonic or ancestral gods, what can be seen and not said, knowledge as immediate—namely *pathos*. The *Libation Bearers* means to show us that one cannot do without the details, the plotting; meaning is impossible without them. This is the significance of what the chorus say in the *Agamemnon* (178, 250), and what proves the underlying principle of tragedy, *pathei mathos*—learning by way of experience or suffering. At the same time, the presence of these details guarantees the imperfection of our knowledge. Seeing may be believing, but it is not knowing. The bloody cloth does not reveal Clytemnestra's guilt. Tragedy puts together the universal and particular in plot—*muthos*—so as to provide us with knowledge of the impossibility of their full togetherness. It reveals to us by way of a *paradeigma*, an example, knowledge of the necessity of our ignorance.[49] It frees us by revealing to us our bondage.

Orestes goes mad at the end of the *Libation Bearers*. He is punished by something only he can see, not by leprosy or pain, but rather by whatever it is that makes him think of them as punishments. The *Libation Bearers* reveals what it means that human beings do not see "things" but

---

49 See Sophocles' *Oedipus Tyrannus*, 1194 and Aristotle's *Rhetoric* Book 2, chapter 20.

things in their significance, things embedded in a story, in a context relative to a soul or souls. "Reality" is always already symbolic—life in a cave. This gets complicated. We see that people often cry when family members die. We then take this to be a sign of their grief, of the state of their souls. We then prescribe crying at funerals so that people understand their own grief poetically as kind of internal crying. All of this is an attempt to get at what is inside, to give it a *logos*. But, as it is the very being of *logos* to point to what is beyond it, *logos* necessarily depends on what it can never completely bring into speech and display. This, the most important thing, eludes it. Aeschylus identifies it with the female. Electra is the true subject of the *Libation Bearers*, but she drops out halfway through, and the play can only be hers if it does not bear her name.

Chapter 2
Sophocles: Electra

Puzzles

In Aeschylus's *Libation Bearers*, Orestes and Electra first meet at line
212. Given Electra's state of mind in the prologue, the meeting seems
unkind in its delay. Nevertheless, it occurs fairly early in the play. In Euripides' *Electra*, the siblings first meet at line 223, a little less than a
sixth of the way through. So here too they come together early in the
play. In Sophocles' version, their meeting does not take place until line
1098 (out of 1510). The delay affects everything, for we are allowed to
see Electra's genuine suffering and sorrow when she presumes Orestes
to be dead. This, along with the lengthening of the time that has elapsed
since Agamemnon's death—it seems to be at least 18 years—allows
Electra to emerge as in some way the paradigm of human suffering
(*pathos*). For Orestes, on the other hand, all experience or suffering of,
all connection to, his home in Argos is hearsay; it is mediated through
logos. Orestes proves to be the paradigm of action. Much more even
than Aeschylus, Sophocles has split apart the two elements of the killing
of Clytemnestra and Aegisthus. These are the two elements of all human
action—on the one hand, motive, emotion, passion and, on the other,
movement, motion, enactment. A just action, like any action, combines
these two, but problematically, for it requires that one have a motive to
act in a way that is neutral. One must be at once divested of one's in-
vestment (disinterested), and invested in this divestment (have an interest
in being disinterested). Electra is invested; her suffering provides her
with motive, but it threatens to make her vengeful rather than just.
Orestes is neutral; his insulation from suffering makes his action potentially fair, but perhaps motiveless, and so impossible. The dramatic puzzle of the play is why Electra and Orestes are separated for so long. Its

thematic puzzle is how what each of the two represents can possibly be brought together.

These problems are connected to another—an odd structural difficulty of the *Electra*. The play is surely Electra's—she speaks about half the 1510 lines and is on stage for all but 86. Her suffering is the theme of the play. While we experience this suffering as a justification for the killing of Clytemnestra and Aegisthus, it plays virtually no role in determining what happens. It is powerful for us, but seems not to affect the action at all. When she hears of Orestes' death, unlike the Electra of the *Libation Bearers* who will not act and so must vanish from the play, this Electra, more manly, resolves to kill Aegisthus with the help of her sister, if possible (954–57), or by herself if necessary (1017–20). However, her action is forestalled by the recognition scene—she needn't act, for Orestes will.

This lack of connection between motive and action emerges in yet another way. While there can be little doubt about Sophocles' skill as a dramaturge, the plot of his *Electra* contains an enormous number of lucky and unexplained coincidences. Can this be accidental? We never learn why this particular chorus is in this particular play—an omission unprecedented in Sophocles' extant plays. It is as though someone had said, "Listen, this is a tragedy. We need a chorus. You're on!" There seems to be no dramatic necessity for their presence. They register their present confidence (479–81) because of what Chrysothemis reports her mother dreamt (417–30), but they offer no interpretation whatsoever of it.[50] The fact of the dream suffices. When Clytemnestra takes the stage, she simply ignores them.

Chrysothemis inadvertently calls our attention to another glitch in the plot. Having been sent by Clytemnestra to offer libations at Agamemnon's

---

50   Chrysothemis adds a new character to the story. She is necessary to the plot, but it is unclear why she could not be the other sister, Iphianassa, originally mentioned in the *Iliad* (9.155, 287) and mentioned in this play by the chorus at line 158. Beginning with Lucretius (*De Rerum Natura* (1.84–101), she is sometimes identified with Iphigenia, whose name is not mentioned in this play, but Sophocles gives no indication that this is the case here. And why, since he is quite aware of Aeschylus's *Oresteia*, would he change her name?

tomb, she reports what she found (892–919) and in the process makes clear to us that had she not been delayed in conversation with Electra (328–471), she would have gotten to the tomb at the same time as Orestes and Pylades, who leave for the tomb at line 85. Had this happened we would have had another play, for had she met Orestes or been told of the signs of his presence before Electra hears of his "death," Electra might have doubted this report.[51]

At the end of the parodos, Orestes sends the *paidagōgos* to do reconnaissance within the palace. When Orestes meets Electra late in the play, she provides him with all the information he needs. Unlike the Orestes of the *Libation Bearers*, this Orestes makes use of his sister, but it is altogether accidental that he does so. This emphasis on the accidental is made quite explicit within the play when, after the recognition scene, the *paidagōgos* emerges from the house and scolds Orestes and Electra for talking to each other so openly and at such length, saying that had he not been watching at the door, word of what they were up to would have gotten out, and their plans would have been thwarted (1326–38). In addition, it is only by accident that Aegisthus is not at home. Orestes could not know this, and he approaches the house before he has heard it from the *paidagōgos*.

So, on its surface, Sophocles' *Electra* seems to be a particularly badly constructed play. Too much depends on chance events—things that just happen to happen, and this despite the fact that the word *kairos*,

---

51 The plotline of the *Electra* is replete with such accidents. The play opens with Orestes, Pylades, and Orestes' *paidagōgos* (childhood protector or tutor). At the end of a short conversation Orestes and Pylades go to Agamemnon's tomb, and the *paidagōgos* to the palace to deliver a message about the death of Orestes. Then Electra and the chorus enter, followed by Chrysothemis, who has been sent to Agamemnon's tomb. Clytemnestra then enters and, after her, the *paidagōgos*, who announces Orestes' death. After Electra decides that it will now be up to her, with or without Chrysothemis, to kill Aegisthus, Orestes and Pylades enter and we have a recognition scene. So, that Electra first mourns Orestes, then resolves to act with Chrysothemis, then resolves to act alone, and finally does not have to act to avenge her father—that is, the plot of the play as a whole depends on the fact that Chrysothemis does not meet Orestes and Pylades at Agamemnon's tomb.

which means something like "just at the right moment," occurs more in this play than in any other of Sophocles' plays.[52] Now, as we have seen, *Electra* is also about the separation of suffering or experience (*pathos*) and action. The play thus runs on two tracks. On the one hand, there are justice and action—represented by Orestes. On the other hand, there are suffering and mourning—represented by Electra. Will the split between Orestes and Electra, and accordingly between the things they represent, have anything to do with Sophocles' atypically "badly" constructed plot?

Prologue: 1–120

The play begins with a speech by the *paidagōgos* addressed to Orestes and describing what he, Orestes, and Pylades see as they enter Mycenae. It is as though he is a tour guide—as though Orestes had never before seen the city. Orestes seems to be an Argive in name only; his attachment to the city is conceptual, not perceptual. This is somehow connected to the strangeness of Pylades' role. Even though he is twice (16, 21) fairly clearly invited to speak (and it would be rather easy to do so since there are only three characters on the stage), Pylades remains silent. Both the *Libation Bearers* and Euripides' *Electra* have complicated recognition scenes, but here Orestes identifies himself only by way of a ring (1223), and no one really recognizes anyone. Pylades, then, seems to be present to remind us of just how anonymous Orestes is in Mycenae. For all we know, he could be Orestes.

Orestes' anonymity is emphasized when the *paidagōgos* speaks of taking him from his sister and bearing him away to care for him (11–13). This was after Agamemnon's murder, and yet the description strongly suggests that Orestes was a baby. Now, Agamemnon returned after having been ten years at Troy. Accordingly, either Orestes is not actually Agamemnon's son, and so the strange anonymity at the outset makes a curious sense, but then what would his motive be in punishing Aegisthus and Clytemnestra? How could we have this play? Or, he is

---

52 *Kairos* occurs seven times in *Electra* (at lines 22, 31, 39, 75, 1259, 1292 and 1368), five times in the *Philoctetes*, four times in *Oedipus the King*, two times in the *Oedipus at Colonus*, one time in the *Trachiniae*, and not at all in *Antigone*.

Agamemnon's son, but then would have to have been at least ten years old when Agamemnon returns and is killed. But then his total lack of familiarity with Mycenae, and so his anonymity and, therefore, his neutrality, would be questionable. So, in the very first speech of the *Electra*, the justice of Orestes has been shown to be problematic. He will prove temporally impossible.

Not just the fact, but details of the tour given by the *paidagōgos* prove significant. He begins with "this is the ancient Argos which you were longing for" (4), and then divides his list of "sights" in two. He first points out a series of Argive landmarks—the sacred ground of Io, not named but called "daughter of Inachus" (5); the *agora* (market-place or assembly-place) of Apollo, not named but called the wolf-killing god (7); and the temple of Hera (8). Now, Zeus had a liaison with Io, whom he then turned into a cow to protect her from Hera's jealousy. When Hera discovers this, she pursues the fleeing Io by way of a gadfly. To be sure, Apollo is the wolf-killing god, but he is also the child of Leto (who could turn herself into a wolf) and Zeus, and so she too was an object of jealousy to Hera. Thus, the three sites cited by the *paidagōgos* are all in some way connected to Hera and call attention to her and her vengeance on those guilty of consorting with Zeus. This is strange, of course, given that Argos is his home by virtue of the marriage of Agamemnon and Clytemnestra, certainly the daughter of Leda, but perhaps also of Zeus disguised as a swan. Hera has a long memory. Should he too not be worried about her jealousy?

The second part of the list of the *paidagōgos* begins with "Say that you see Mycenae" (9)—not Argos. Orestes must "say" that he sees them because the *paidagōgos* proceeds to cite two "sights" that are not sites, but things Orestes cannot possibly see—the bloody history of the house of the sons of Pelops (unlike the *Libation Bearers*, this play gives us no indication that Orestes' action will bring this bloody history to an end)[53]

---

53 He could have referred not to the Pelopids—Pelops really acted in self-defense when he killed Oenomaus—but to the Tantalids—Tantalus attempted to feed his son, Pelops, to the gods. The *paidagōgos* thus avoids mentioning the most unjust of the deeds of the house and, of course, also does not mention that we cannot assume that Orestes, as the last of this house, will avoid the injustice that characterizes its bloody deeds.

and the renown of Mycenae for its wealth. The *paidagōgos* thus couples the prosperity of Mycenae with its murderousness and thereby calls into question the conventional connection between wealth and happiness.

After his tour, the *paidagōgos* goes on to tell Orestes that he raised him for one purpose alone, so that upon arriving at manhood he would be the avenger of his father (13–14).[54] And yet, shockingly, Orestes has told him nothing about what Apollo's oracle has told him to do. The *paidagōgos* ends his opening speech by telling Orestes and Pylades to "deliberate" (16) and "join together in speeches" (21) so that they may settle on a course of action. Apparently, he has no idea why they are in Mycenae. On the one hand, he must think Orestes rather slow since the three are in front of the house, day is just breaking, and they are in a vulnerable situation, but as far as he knows they have made no plan at all. On the other hand, the three have been on the road for some time, Orestes has carried a funeral urn all the way from Phocis and has only just now hidden it in a bush, but it has never occurred to the *paidagōgos* to ask why. It seems fair to wonder who is the slow one here.

Orestes begins his response by likening the *paidagōgos*, the man who reared him from childhood, to an old well-born horse. It is the first sign of condescension only thinly clothed in respect. Pylades does not accept the invitation to deliberate because he seems to know that, based on the oracle, Orestes has already made his decision about what to do. The elder *paidagōgos* is the very junior partner in this conspiracy. Orestes' plan of action is based on the instructions of the oracle. But as in the *Libation Bearers*, we do not hear the words of the oracle; we rather get Orestes' interpretation of their meaning.[55] We do not even know what question he put to the oracle. He might well have asked, "How am I to kill my mother?" and not, "Am I to kill my mother?" The oracle tells Orestes to do the killing by stealth and not openly. Later Orestes adds that he was also told to do the sacred things for his father. But these two

---

54   The *paidagōgos* says nothing about justice. In his reply, Orestes mentions it only when speaking of the oracle. Apart from this, we are given no indication initially that Orestes is motivated by revenge, only that he longs to see his home.

55   Phoebus gave Orestes an oracle in this sort of way (*toiauth'* 35).

parts of the oracle are not clearly compatible, for the doing of the sacred things might compromise secrecy.

This tension is prefigured at the end of the opening speech of the *paidagōgos*, where, on the one hand he urges that they "join together in speeches" (21) and on the other hand says that this is the perfect moment (*kairos*) for action (22). As in the *Libation Bearers*, talk, *logos*, is at odds with action.[56] This tension is connected as well to the fact that no one mentions Electra until she is heard moaning. There is no indication that Orestes means to include her in their plan even though there are clearly ways in which she might get in the way if she were not to know. And we are soon to learn from Electra (169–72) that Orestes has been regularly sending messages to her. Why does he not send one last message to tell her he is coming? Does he not trust her? The significance of this omission is clear when Orestes charges the *paidagōgos* with the task of going into the house to gain information (38–43). Orestes assures him that it has been so long since they left that no one will recognize him (42–43), but is this really the case? Suppose the *paidagōgos* was between 40 and 50 when Electra put Orestes in his arms. He would now be between 60 and 70. Do people become unrecognizable when aging in this way?[57] Why does Orestes not send Pylades instead of the *paidagōgos* and avoid this problem? Or why not contact Electra? She is the one who ends up giving him the information he needs despite his plan, and he has been in touch with her regularly. While it is true that in order to show Electra's grief at the death of her brother, she cannot have recognized him, this is a necessity of the plot, not of the action itself. For whatever reason, the *paidagōgos* is made central to the plan. The immediate consequence is that, having just heard the moaning of Electra, when Orestes asks him whether they should remain, the *paidagōgos* says that they should not—that pouring libations at Agamemnon's tomb first

---

56 *Logos* occurs five times in Orestes' speech (30, 44, 56, 59, and 63). Three of the five are used to describe the account of his death—he is dead in speech, but not in deed.

57 Euripides clearly doesn't agree with Orestes; in his *Electra* (631) he indicates that none of the servants in Aegisthus's house have ever seen Orestes. Apparently, those who might have been inclined to support a restoration have all been purged.

will assure their victory. This assertion links the two parts of the oracle by making the success of their action hinge on their piety—i.e., what they "say" in advance of their action.

But is this Orestes' view? Orestes tells the *paidagōgos* to lie and to swear an oath to the truth of what he has said. Rather than doing so, the *paidagōgos* gives an elaborate version of the story of Orestes' death that runs on for eighty-three lines (680–763). He substitutes detail for swearing.[58] It seems strange that the demands of religion are enforced by the *paidagōgos*, the man not privy to the plan that depends on religion. Orestes is not worried about the consequences of using religion in this way. How can he be harmed by being dead in *logos* while alive in deed (59–60)? After all, no utterance accompanied by gain is bad, and many after being thought dead (i.e., being dead in *logos*), when they come home receive great honor (61–64).[59] What then is Orestes' goal in returning? It does not seem to be revenge, nor to come to the aid of Electra, nor—despite the *paidagōgos* account—a yearning to see his homeland. Orestes returns for the sake of ruling his wealth and of setting his house straight (71–72). Justice is getting back what is his own, understood largely in terms of his wealth. Now, the problem of the play is the tension between motive (Electra) and objectivity (Orestes as dispenser of justice). And yet, as a character in a drama, Orestes must have a motive for his actions. Accordingly, Sophocles has provided him with the shallowest, the least emotive, of possible motives.

This is connected to Orestes' understanding of gain by way of *logos*, and so of the power of poetry. His whole plan, in terms of evidence, depends on the funeral urn. It presupposes great piety on the part of Clytemnestra—i.e., that she will find it unimaginable that anyone would have the gall to fake funeral rites. Aegisthus, on the other hand, when he returns home, thinks that he is going to see the body of Orestes. Had

---

58 In Aeschylus's *Agamemnon* (281–350), after Clytemnestra first announces the fall of Troy to the chorus, she tells them about the series of signal fires that allows her to know. They are skeptical. Then she provides them with an account filled with particular details of the victory of the Greeks and the suffering of the Trojans, details that she cannot possibly know, and they believe her.

59 This has interesting implications for the power of poetry.

he been told that he would encounter Orestes' ashes, he might well have been suspicious. Electra, like her mother, takes the ashes to be Orestes, and mourns his death accordingly. Electra and Clytemnestra are in this regard alike—both pious; and this piety is grounded in their trust in *logos*. That the *paidagōgos* substitutes elaborate *logos* for an oath is perhaps no accident. The fake funeral urn is like *logos* purified—it points only to itself and is subject to no underlying reality.

The prologue postpones the recognition scene (82) and so makes possible Electra's mourning of Orestes. This, in turn, makes possible the scene between Electra and Chrysothemis in which Electra tests her sister's mettle with respect to the killing of their mother. Chrysothemis is revealed as the weak sister, but why is this necessary for the plot? Chrysothemis's unwillingness to participate in the murder allows Electra to show how she herself has changed. Her sister challenges Electra by saying that if she was old enough all those years ago to spirit Orestes away, she was already an adult and so able to have killed their mother as well. This enables us to see that, while she may now be willing to kill Clytemnestra, for twenty years Electra has been pushing matricide from her mind. This transformation of Electra is somehow the most powerful feature of the play named for her. And yet, still, Electra's transformation will have virtually no effect on the action of the play.

Hearing Electra moan, Orestes, Pylades, and the *paidagōgos* exit (77–85), and Electra gives her first extended speech (86–120). It divides in two—a speech about mourning (86–102) and a speech about vengeance (103–120). Once again, the principle is *logos* versus *ergon*, speech versus deed. It is meant to introduce the *kommos* that will take the place of a *parados* (121–250), of which the issue will also be mourning versus vengeance. In the section on mourning, we find Electra doing what she always does—she is in a constant state of mourning (103–09), although this turns out to be true only when Aegisthus is absent.[60] Electra's mourning has to do not with Agamemnon's death itself, but with the manner of his death. She would not have regrets had he died at Troy,

---

60 It is not clear that Electra's mourning is constant in any case. Lines 86–95 suggest that she may mourn only in the day, or at least first by day and then, after some interruption, by night.

but she mourns the fact that he was killed by Clytemnestra and Aegisthus. What is clear is that she holds her pity unique because of the constancy of her mourning (100–01).

The order of her behavior is reversed in the section on the call to vengeance, which begins at night. Pity seems to move from day (or happiness) to night (or sorrow), while vengeance moves from night/sorrow to day/happiness. Electra thus presents vengeance as an escape from grief or pain (117–20). But she presents the grief from which it is to be an escape in a very strange way. She alludes to it by way of the songstress, the nightingale, and gives the nightingale the epithet *teknoleteira* (107). This should mean "destroying (or slaying) the young," which is how Lloyd-Jones translates it, but others resist this translation. David Grene translates it as "robbed of her young," and interprets it freely as the "ravished nest" of the nightingale.[61] This disagreement is possible because the word seems to occur only here in extant Greek texts. And yet, the ambiguity may be the point. On the one hand, Electra presents herself as one who has lost her child (although it remains unclear why Agamemnon should be likened to her child). On the other hand, she presents herself as one who has killed her own child, that is, as akin to Agamemnon. This is all connected to the story of Philomela, the nightingale. Procne (swallow) kills her son Itys (pheasant) and feeds him to his father Tereus (hoopoe) as punishment because Tereus raped her sister, Philomela, and cut out her tongue so that she could not tell anyone of the rape. Electra, then, likens herself to a mother who is in constant lamentation for the child she killed to avenge her sister.[62] Her lamentation, therefore, involves an admixture of guilt. The point of invoking the story of Philomela seems to be that the intrusion of justice into mourning makes the burden of mourning overwhelming. And this leads not exactly to a longing for justice, but rather to a longing for a

---

61 Hugh Lloyd-Jones, trans., *Sophocles I* (Cambridge, MA and London: Harvard University Press, 1997), 177; David Grene and Richmond Lattimore, eds., *Sophocles II* (Chicago and London: University of Chicago Press, 1969), 130; R. Store, *Sophocles II* (Cambridge, MA and London: Harvard University Press and William Heineman Ltd.), 135.

62 Agamemnon, of course, killed his own daughter in order to be able to avenge a crime committed against his brother, Menelaus.

release from the pain of constant lamentation. And this release requires revenge. The plot of the play is therefore set up as a conflict of passion. Electra introduces Orestes as a possible avenger who will in his act of vengeance release her from pain.

All of this has to do with an issue familiar to us from the *Libation Bearers*. Toward the end of her speech (110–17) the goal at which Electra aims is presented as requiring three sorts of divine intervention—by Olympian gods concerned with justice (Hades and Persephone), the in-between god (chthonic Hermes), and the chthonic, personal, inner gods (Curse and Furies). Electra does not see herself as taking on guilt in the aftermath of the vengeance she seeks. She rather sees herself as doing what must be done to release herself from inner torment. The issue might be put this way. The chorus are about to come in and ask Electra what the connection is between the two things she seems to want—vengeance and lamentation. It is as though they ask her, "Why are we having this play?" What is it that connects suffering with striking back, and why should the latter bring release from the former?

Sophocles' *Electra* divides in three parts. The first is half of the prologue and belongs to Orestes (1–85). The second is the bulk of the play and belongs to Electra (86–1094). In the third, the remainder of the play (1095–510), Orestes and Electra are together. The action of the play, the killing of Clytemnestra and Aegisthus, only really requires the first and third parts. Nothing would change if the second were omitted altogether, and yet it is the most interesting of the parts. It is as though Sophocles watched Aeschylus's *Libation Bearers*, noticed that Electra drops out of the play at line 509, and asked, "What is she doing during the rest of the play?" Sophocles makes the *pathos* of Electra the issue by making it seem as though it can be utterly separated from the action. He does that by making Orestes' motive as superficial as possible. Sophocles begins the play by forcing us to see that Orestes is impossible. He must be both a baby and ten years old when the *paidagōgos* receives him from Electra. We find ourselves assuming the first, that he was a baby and pure. The second part of the play, Electra's part, is designed to articulate for us what it means that this purity is impossible—that to be what he is, Orestes must also have been ten.

As we have seen, this is connected to the curious way in which nothing fits together in this *Electra*. Things without which the whole plot would collapse seem to happen by chance. So, on the one hand, Electra will give a powerful lamentation over Orestes' ashes, but he is not really dead; he is standing right next to her. While the *paidagōgos* will give a powerful account of Orestes' death in a chariot race, none of it is true. Aegisthus will return home and gloat over what he assumes is Orestes' corpse, but it proves not to be Orestes' but that of Clytemnestra. On the other hand, Orestes will kill his mother without showing any emotion. He emerges after the killing and, in response to Electra's question about how he fared, he responds "in the house beautifully" (1424–25). And the play, which begins with birds singing (18), will end not with furies chasing Orestes, but with the chorus claiming that Orestes' freedom has been perfected by the day's deed (1508–10). In the prologue we are introduced to this split between passion with no link to reality and real deeds that are passionless. The split leaves us with the impression that the play is not put together very well, but what we have begun to see is the possibility that this split between *pathos*/passion/suffering and *ergon*/deed/action is the whole point. Unlike the *Libation Bearers* and Euripides' *Electra*, these two elements are not brought together until quite late. This problem of the play's structure is an image of the problem the play means to think through.

We saw that the split between Orestes as the representative of action and Electra as the representative of passion shows up in Electra's first speech as the problem of the connection between vengeance and grief. What exactly is it about vengeance that serves to relieve one's grief? Why should this be the case? When we suffer a very specific loss that wounds us, without our quite realizing, this affects our whole view of the world. A world in which chance can play such a nasty trick on us looks very gloomy. In this way a specific wound may give way to a general nihilism. Grief feeds on itself, but in doing so it begins to leave its initial cause behind. This is Electra. But with the possibility of revenge, it seems as though the specificity of the wound can be restored by way of a specific response to it—tit for tat. Vengeance restores our sense of being in control and not at the mercy of chance. Of course, in its way, nihilism was also an attempt to regain control; by utterly lowering our expectations of justice, we cannot be harmed by chance—it can't take us unawares. As the chorus suggest in the last lines of the play, then, grief and vengeance have a common root—the attempt to reassert our freedom in the face of chance.

The Parados: *121–250*

The *parodos* takes the form of a *kommos*, an exchange between Electra and the chorus about her constant grieving. As we have seen, that we are given no idea who this chorus are or why they are present, is unprecedented in the extant plays of Sophocles.[63] The *parodos* divides into three strophic systems, each strophe and each antistrophe with one exchange between Electra and the chorus, and an *epode*.

In the first strophe (121–36) the chorus begin with an emphasis on the fact that Electra always (*aei*, 122) mourns—that her mourning is unceasing, insatiable (*akorestos*, 123). They have heard it all before and seem a bit tired of what has become in Electra more a constant disposition than a reaction to a specific event. Still, while we don't know why, they do take her side. Yet they seem more concerned (and this will hold true for them throughout) with the manner than the fact of Agamemnon's death (124–26). They end by calling for the one doing *tade* (either "these things" or "in this way") to perish "if it is *themis* (right according to the gods) for me to utter *tade*" (127). On the surface, at least, they are not sure. At the very beginning of the *parodos*, then, the chorus raise the question implicit in Electra's previous speech: "What is the connection between grief and vengeance?" In her response, Electra, not for the last time, altogether misunderstands their intent. They say, "Cut it out; enough is enough." Rather perversely, she takes their "always" and "insatiable" as a compliment to the completeness and perfection of her misery, and responds, "Thank you for the consolation."

In the antistrophe, the chorus once again point out that Electra is ever wailing in lamentation (141) and add that there is no way that what she is doing will have any possible consequences. It will not raise

---

63 Electra will address the chorus as *genethla gennaiōs* (129) one nobly born of those of noble birth. They are not slaves, and Electra measures their nobility, and so perhaps her own, by their parentage.

Agamemnon from the dead.[64] There is no way of undoing evils. What then is the point of Electra's behavior? As yielding nothing, no good, it cannot really be called an action; to engage in this act of inaction is to be immoderate. Grief generally, they say, is a reaction to being device-less (*amēchanos*,140), and so without hope. And finally, why should Electra go after or yearn for the unbearable things with *them*—why in-volve them in all of this (143)?

Electra begins her response with an interesting choice of words. "Foolish (*nēpios*) [is] he who is forgetful of the piteously departed par-ents." (144–45). *Nēpios* here is surely to be taken metaphorically. Origi-nally it means "not yet speaking" and so an "infant"; from this it becomes "childish," and then "foolish." If we read it more literally, Electra would be saying that one who forgets or neglects parents who have suffered pitiable deaths is a baby who has no speech. On the one hand, of course, this would be Orestes—handed over to the *paidagōgos* as a baby. On the other hand, it would be all children. But, since the obvious reading of *nē-pios* here is the metaphoric "foolish," this would mean we are all built in this foolish way. You have to be a parent not to forget, to have your life totally invested in others—your children, your *genethla*.[65] Accordingly, Electra cites Procne and Niobe as examples—both mothers, and both re-sponsible for the deaths of the children they mourn.[66] In Procne and Niobe, mourning and revenge are one because by being miserable they hurt the doers of the deeds they mourn—they hurt themselves. Electra calls Niobe, transformed into a rock that forever spills water or tears, a god. To be a god means to be eternally in a single mode, to forever func-tion in a manifest way as Niobe cries and Procne, as a swallow, ever sings the song "itus, itus." In using them as paradigms for her own mourning, Electra betrays her intent. Knowingly or no, she wishes to turn herself into a poetic figure, a god. However, unlike Niobe and Procne, her two

64 That they deny this possibility out of hand and that Electra has called them nobly born distinguishes them from the chorus of the *Libation Bearers*.

65 See Clytemnestra's reaction to the "death" of Orestes at 770.

66 Procne boils Itys and feeds him to Tereus, her husband, to punish him for the rape of her sister, Philomela. Niobe boasts of her children in comparison to those of Leto, a goddess. The gods punish her by killing them. Zeus then turns her into a rock from which water, tears, constantly flow.

parts are not so easily unified. On the one hand, she mourns; on the other hand, she demands justice. It is not clear how the two are to be made one.

The chorus begin the second strophe (153–72) by chiding Electra. She is not unique. Distress is manifest among all mortals and even more so among those linked by blood, as Electra is linked to Chrysothemis, Iphianassa, and Orestes.[67] Having introduced the question of blood ties, and so of generation, the chorus then say that Orestes, hidden in youth from these painful things, will at some time (*pote*), on account of his ancestry, be received by the earth of Mycenae (161–63). On the one hand then, Electra has been identified with perpetual grief, which necessarily unfolds in time. On the other hand, Electra wants justice, which does not make sense in terms of time. If the gods are willing to grant justice, why do they not simply strike down evil at once, at the moment it occurs, or why even allow it to occur at all? The compatibility of justice and grief seems problematic. In the plot of the *Electra*, the contingency that postpones this dilemma is Orestes; he is not simply one, but changes—he had to grow up. But Orestes is now grown. So where is he? What is the reason for the delay? The problem for Electra is in some way the same as the problem of why the chorus are present. Sophocles writes a play in which there seems no reason for the chorus or the play itself to happen now, and uses this contingency as an entrée to the question of what it would mean to mix together justice and time.

Electra responds to this problem first in terms of the constancy of sorrow. Hers is unwearying (*akamata*, 164). She always (*aiein*) drips

---

67 Chrysothemis and Iphianassa (who is never mentioned again in the play) are both mentioned at *Iliad* 9.145–48 where, with another daughter, Laodike (whose name means something like "justice of the people"), Agamemnon offers any of the three in marriage to Achilles if he will return to the fighting. It is curious that both Electra and Iphigenia are not in Homer unless Iphigenia is the same as Iphianassa (Clytemnestra will refer to the sacrifice of Electra's sister at 532, but she never names her) and Electra is the same as Laodike (in which case, Sophocles, having called our attention to the *Iliad*, would have called our attention as well to removing the connection between Electra and justice). But these identities are difficult, since it would be strange to draw attention here to the common distress of siblings and include Iphigenia.

tears (165). Her doom of ills is endless (*anēnuton*, 166). Of Orestes, she says that "on the one hand, he always longs, but, on the other hand, while longing, he does not deem it worth it to appear" (1171–72). How then does the "always" of sorrow turn into the "now" of action? Electra's description of herself makes her like Niobe (152), like a god. She presents her sorrow as being born of having no children and being unwed.[68] For Electra, there is no generation—she is not in time—but her godhood is like that of *chronos*, "time" but also a pun on Kronos, or of *ouranos*, "heaven." It is a constant function. Electra's question then, the question of the compatibility of justice and time, is a version of the problematic nature of gods generally, but especially of the Olympians: How is Zeus (or for that matter, Christ) possible? How is a god, who is not simply a constant but a person, who, for example is not simply Ares as war, but an Ares who at a certain time commits adultery with Aphrodite, possible? How can a god enter into time? How is it possible for Zeus to determine the moment when Orestes comes home (162–63)?

The problem of Sophocles' *Electra* is a rethinking of the problem of Aeschylus's *Oresteia*—how to mix together the chthonic, inner, and permanent character of the divine with the Olympian, active, and temporal character of the divine. What connects the Furies, understood as inner guilt, with the Furies as external agents, and finally, as legal guilt? What is it that is common to and connects the "female" (and so Electra) with the male (Orestes)? It is possible to account for the delay of meting out justice, and therefore for the imperfection of justice in the world, by way of the willfulness of the Olympian gods. When gods are understood not simply to represent permanent functions and features of the world, but are agents, persons, who have purposes of their own and therefore can even be appealed to for assistance with prayer and sacrifice, it becomes possible to account for injustice by way of our incomplete understanding of their purposes. This points to a fundamental tension between what we may call the permanent and atemporal structure of justice or right, a relation of fixed principles, and so the being of justice, and the necessarily temporal experience of justice, its coming to be, or *genesis*.

68 Her name derives from *ēlektros*, meaning "amber," but easily gives rise to the pun *alektros*, meaning "unwed" or "unbedded."

This tension between being and becoming is the explicit theme of the second antistrophe of the parados (174–92). Zeus, the Olympian, is great in *ouranos*, heaven (175–76). The chorus, therefore, tell Electra to be patient, to distribute, or perhaps farm out, her anger to Zeus.[69] She is urged to realize that Zeus has his own purposes, for time, *chronos* (and, by pun, Kronos), is a god who brings ease. So, all three of the generations of the gods—Ouranos, his son Kronos, and his son Zeus—are present, and in the account of the chorus, they are united in their purpose. Like heaven, Zeus looks over everything, and yet everything is not static, for time too is one of the permanent things, i.e., a god. The chorus thus urge an appreciation of the permanence of change. Accordingly, they end by claiming neither Orestes, who will determine the future, nor Hades, who rules over the dead, the past, will fail to heed Electra. Still, Electra responds that while that is all very well, she does not have unlimited time. Her life passes; what is the overall pattern of change to her? She wants justice in time.

The third strophe (193–212) begins with the chorus further reflecting on the split between the pattern of justice and the enactment of justice, between the permanent and the contingent, being and coming to be. They wish to be concerned with the former rather than the latter, and so they again emphasize the manner rather than the fact of Agamemnon's death (193–200). The one showing it forth or making it known (*phrasas*[70]) was cunning, but *eros* was the killer. Together "they" engendered a *deinos* form in a *deinos* way, whether understood as divine or mortal, uncanny or canny. On the one hand, then, the agents were mortal. "They" are Clytemnestra and Aegisthus, who were cunning in executing their plan. On the other hand, the deed was inevitable given the permanent structure of things, the very nature of their erotic longing. Clytemnestra and Aegisthus were apparently effects, not causes. The chorus unwittingly call attention not only to the character of this deed, the killing of Agamemnon, but of all human doing. Looking forward, planning our

---

69 The verb is *nemein* and means "to apportion," but also as "to graze" it is cognate with *nomos*—law.

70 Lloyd-Jones translates *phrasas* as "teacher." Grene has "contriver," Kells "devised," and Storr "conceived."

actions, we must think ourselves free agents, able to do what we decide to do. Looking back at our actions and seeking to understand what we have done, we cannot do other than try to articulate them in terms of permanent principles. In understanding, what we wanted to do becomes what we had to do. This, the *deinos* shape of all human action as both canny and uncanny, when unself-aware, is the structure of tragedy. Electra responds (201–12) first by situating her father's death in a certain time, and then by calling upon Zeus to make his killers suffer and asking that they should not at any time avail themselves of splendors in doing such deeds. In this way she confirms Zeus as the principle of the permanent entering into time.

In the third antistrophe (213–32), the chorus ask Electra if she is so unaware of what sort of things the present comes from that she plunges to her own ruin (214–16). They think she does not understand what it means to exist in time. Rebuking her for "always engendering wars in [her] melancholy soul" (218–19), they tell her not to challenge those in power. Now, *tois dunatois* certainly means those in power, but it may also mean "potencies," "possibilities" or "contingencies." Whether it refers here to Clytemnestra and Aegisthus or to the Olympians, it also seems to point to agency as what is at odds with permanence. In her response Electra once more takes what was meant as a rebuke as consolation. The chorus tell her she should not always be mourning. She should exercise some restraint and so, by acting, curtail her lamentation. But Electra does not think she is a serial mourner. She rather thinks that she is her mourning. She claims she was compelled to do *deinos* things by *deinos* things, for her laments are without number. This means twice defining herself (226, 231) as not at any time consolable. There is considerable irony in her response, for she asks the chorus how she could hear a suitable word from someone thinking in a way just at the right time (*kairia*) (226–28). Apparently thinking about the necessity of timeless permanence, must still partake of the contingent and time-bound. Electra needs to think herself permanent as a means of consoling herself in her impermanence.

The chorus begin the epode (233–50) by assuring Electra that they speak with good will, like a trustworthy mother, and so advise her not to engender distress by way of distress. They think that Electra has generated a second order of temporality, and indeed she has. She does not mourn; she thinks of herself as mourning. In a way, Electra is ritual mourning. We have seen this before—nihilism as a temporal effort to freeze temporality and thus control chance. If everything is equally and predictably bad, then nothing ever really changes. We take comfort in the fact that we can count on our misery. Electra concludes the parados by confirming this second order temporality. As much as she attempts to make herself like a chthonic deity, misery in its permanent and unchanging form, Electra cannot avoid the language of nature and growth:

> And what measure of badness grows? Come, how [is] it beautiful (*kalon*) to have no care for those having passed away? Among whom of human beings does this bloom? (236–40)

The First Episode: 251–471

If the theme of the *parados* is the permanence of Electra's grief, the first episode begins with the reasons for this grief (251–327). After the chorus pretty much openly admit that they have no particular reason to be present,[71] Electra follows suit by saying "force compels [her] to do these things" (256). Her first reason for her perpetual grieving, then, does not shed any light—she simply claims that this is who she is. Her second reason is also problematic. Electra asks how a well-born woman could do anything other than she has done but, of course, Chrysothemis (not to mention Iphianassa) is as well-born as Electra, and she has not followed Electra's path. After these reasons, seven more particular reasons follow. Electra points to her enmity with her mother (261–62), to her life in her own home among her father's murderers (263–64)[72], to their rule over her with respect to what she is given and denied (264–65), to seeing Aegisthus

---

71 "On the one hand, I have come for our interests, both yours and mine; on the other, if I do not speak beautifully, you be victorious, for we will follow." (251–53).

72 Or a less likely, but interesting, reading that she lives "in the house among the murderers of me and of the father."

on her father's throne (267–68), to seeing him wear her father's clothes (268–69), to seeing him sacrifice at the hearth where he killed Agamemnon (269–70),[73] and to seeing the final act of the hybris of Clytemnestra and Aegisthus—their lying together on her father's bed (271–73). But clearly Electra has gotten carried away with her description. She almost certainly did not see this final act of hybris. She has moved from what she has actually seen to what she imagines having seen. But the seamlessness of this transition calls into question the straightforward veracity of the rest of her account. Electra's imagination governs her mourning.[74]

The first part of Electra's speech (254–74) moves from Clytemnestra to "them" to Aegisthus, but in the second part of her speech (275–309), she returns to Clytemnestra. Aegisthus is merely a digression from her major point—her hatred of her mother. In this speech, Electra has essentially written a play in order to display her misery. Here her emphasis on Clytemnestra's continued celebration of Agamemnon's death suggests that Electra understands Clytemnestra too to keep her vengeance alive. Her mother laughs (277) and sets up *choroi* (280)—either dances or choruses (so, she too produces plays?). She sacrifices to the gods (281) and holds feasts bearing Agamemnon's name (283–35)—the two are, of course, not simply different since the meat of the cattle sacrificed would be eaten by those attending. Living with (*suneinai*), literally "being with" (which in Greek, as in English, may mean to engage in sexual intercourse with) Aegisthus might well also be a way of extending Clytemnestra's punishment of Agamemnon. Every time she has sex with Aegisthus, she punishes Agamemnon for the sacrifice of their daughter. This suggests that Clytemnestra needs Electra to remind her of what she did, to renew her sense of having been wronged. Vengeance has not allayed her grief over the death of her daughter. Were Electra paying attention, she would notice that Clytemnestra is proof that her longing to be relieved of her grief will not be satisfied by the death of her mother.

Accordingly, Electra's speech makes us question her judgment. Everything she quotes Clytemnestra as having said about Orestes can

73 So, Clytemnestra did not kill her husband in his bath?
74 Euripides will highlight this problem in his Electra. See lines 160–65 and 300–338.

be read in a double way. Clytemnestra could, for example, blame Electra for stealing Orestes out of her arms (295–97) because it put her in danger, but she could also mean to blame Electra for alienating her from her son. If Orestes was a mere baby, Aegisthus would have been the only father he ever knew. Everything Electra said about the throne, the clothing, as well as her remarks about how infants forget their parents (145–46), points to this. In addition, when Electra questions Aegisthus's manliness because he goes into battle with the help of women, and in the sequel laments that Orestes has not come—presumably she plans to aid him when he does—she reveals herself to be much more like Clytemnestra than she is willing to acknowledge.

The second part of the first episode (328–471) is an exchange between Electra and her sister Chrysothemis. It divides into two sections, each of which in turn divides in two. In the first section (328–404) they first speak of what divides the two of them (328–75) and second of the new plans that Aegisthus and Clytemnestra have for Electra (376–404). The second section first deals with an account of Clytemnestra's dream (405–430) and second moves to Electra's call to thwart Clytemnestra's plan on the level of ritual (431–71). In each of these two-fold divisions the ordering principle is the relation between passion and action, between suffering and its just remedy, between what is happening to Electra and what is to be done.[75] What is strange, and interesting, is that the agreement of Electra and Chrysothemis about what to do on the level of ritual (what is to be done at the tomb of Agamemnon) does not bring with it an agreement on the nature of Electra's suffering. Accordingly, we get a rehearsal of an old quarrel between them about the fruitlessness of Electra's endless lamentation, a quarrel that Chrysothemis even admits being unnecessary to rehash (373–74). She justifies reraising the issue of lamentation because of the plan Clytemnestra and Aegisthus have to imprison Electra, genuinely wishing to warn her sister; but Chrysothemis also wants to use this new evidence to triumph in their perennial argument and to demonstrate that she has been right from the beginning.

75 So that 251–327:328–471::328–404:405–471::328–375:376–404::405–430:431–471.

Their argument looks as though it pits total and timeless adherence to principle against the temporal flexibility of common sense.[76] Still the sisters share something; they do what they do in the name of freedom.[77] However, for Chrysothemis freedom requires compromise (339–40), while Electra counters that she is not really free, for she speaks nothing from herself (341–44). Electra makes the conflict one of *logos* versus *ergon*—word versus deed: "I pain them. . . . With me, you hate, but the hating is in word, while in deed you are with those who murdered your father" (356–57). This split between Electra and Chrysothemis, which in form and in content dominates their entire interchange, reproduces the split made manifest in the roles of Orestes and Electra. In doing so it distinguishes two forms of suffering—active passion and passive passion. In a revealingly ambiguous sentence, Electra says *tēs sēs d'ouk erō timēs lachein* (364).[78] It most obviously means "But I do not love to obtain (or hit upon) your honor." But if *erō* were read not as "I love" but as its homonym "I will speak," it would mean "But I will not speak to obtain your honor." The two possible readings remind us of the chorus's earlier claim (197) that the speaker was guile and the killer eros. Here (369–71) that makes clear that the goal is to put the two together—Electra and Chrysothemis, loving and speaking.

In the second section of the second part of the episode, they turn to Clytemnestra's dream. Chrysothemis relates the dream that she heard from someone present when Clytemnestra tells it to the sun.

There is a *logos* of her beholding a father, both yours and mine, coming into the light—together again a second time.

---

76 This reminds us of the argument between Antigone and Ismene at the very beginning of *Antigone* (1–99).

77 Once again, they are like the sisters in *Antigone*, who share a loyalty to family even if Antigone's is to the one into which she was born into while Ismene's is to the one she will potentially generate. See Seth Benardete, *Sacred Transgressions: A Reading of Sophocles'* Antigone (South Bend IN: St. Augustine's Press, 1999), 9.

78 Some manuscripts substitute *tuchein*, to happen or chance, for *lachein*; see Lloyd-Jones and Wilson, *Sophoclis Fabulae* (Oxford: Oxford University Press, 1990), 74. It does not greatly alter the sense.

Then, he took a scepter he himself at one time bore, but now
Aegisthus [bears], to plant at the hearth. And from this shot
up a teeming shoot, by which all the land of Mycenae came
to be shaded. (417–23)

The dream would surely not be difficult to interpret—Orestes is born
from the scepter, which is rightfully his father's, and comes to rule over
all the land—but as it is never given an interpretation, we are left to conclude that the mere fact of the dream is sufficient to terrify Clytemnestra.
A nighttime fear moves Clytemnestra to send Electra into eternal darkness (379) and to offer burnt offerings and send libations to the tomb of
Agamemnon (426–27), but how are these two responses connected? In
Clytemnestra's nighttime fear Electra finds a sign that the gods have at
last come to her aid (411). What is important is not the potential ambiguity of her mother's inner turmoil but the fact that it serves unambiguously as punishment. Apparently, justice allows of no ambiguity. This
is connected to Chrysothemis's parting remark: "For it is not possible
for a pair to contest a just *logos* but to hasten the doing onward." (466–
67). Because a just *logos* is perfectly clear, deed supersedes speech.
Agamemnon came once more into the light. Electra will be placed per-
manently in the dark. Clytemnestra's dream, the sign of her inner state,
needs no interpretation. The chthonic gods have been replaced by the
Olympians. Electra's lamentation is now to be understood not as the sign
of inner mourning, but as external punishment. Her passion, her non-
action, is now an action designed to cause her mother to suffer. This is
the consequence of the second order temporality in which Electra enacts
her passivity. And this, in turn, has something to do with the power of
acting understood as a kind of faking to affect acting understood as
doing.

Second Thoughts

Sophocles' *Electra* is the story of the chorus that is there for no reason.
This is perhaps the first sign that things in the play do not seem to fit together very well. Apollo told Orestes to do two things, leave libations at
his father's tomb and kill his father's killers stealthily, but no connection

is made between the two and, indeed, they turn out to be at odds. Clytemnestra has a dream and changes her mind about what to do about Electra but, again, no connection between the two is made explicit. Was it because of the dream that she changed her mind? There is no reason why Chrysothemis doesn't meet Orestes at their father's tomb. There is no reason why she doesn't get back to speak with Electra before the *paidagōgos* announces Orestes' "death." Nor is there a reason why Aegisthus is not at home. We get a long account of the cause of Orestes' death, which might have been true, but is not. Similarly, the corpse that Aegisthus comes back to view might have been that of Orestes, but is not. All of this suggests that the problem of causality is at the heart of *Electra*. Between one event and another it is always possible to squeeze in a third that would alter the flow in time. So, we never have certainty that a particular event will be the cause of another. This dissociation of events in *Electra* is simply an exaggerated version of a necessary feature of our lives, of any lives, in time. In the *Electra*, we experience not causality, but contiguity.

But what has this to do with the content of the play—matricide? In *Electra*, we have a character who approaches total passivity. She does not act. She is acted upon and is altogether passive in the face of what happens. Clytemnestra will say that this constant lamentation shames Electra's *philoi*—her friends or kin (518). Is this ultimately the shame of not being an agent, of being totally passive? And yet, is there any alternative to this passivity in a world where we experience only sequence and not cause? In a way, Electra seems to be waiting for Godot. *Electra* presents a story in which Electra's passivity brings us, its audience, to accept the view on which it is based. We accept a plot with insufficient causality and pretend that everything is in order. Then Electra is brought finally to renounce her passivity, to decide that she alone will murder Aegisthus (she never says she will kill her mother), only to have Orestes intervene and "save the day" so that her will comes to naught. In the end, Electra is passive. Is this true as well of us who were seduced to passivity by accepting the lack of causality in the plot?

The various longings for *dikē* (whether as justice or as punishment) in *Electra* suggest that it is at its core a longing to end the sequence of tit for tat events—the curse on the house. It is a longing for a final result, for closure, that moves human beings to act. We want to experience in time the atemporal reason for these tit for tat actions that unfold in time. This, of course, is not possible. The finality is illusory. The great irony of the play that becomes clear in the first stasimon and the second episode, is that in her hatred of Clytemnestra, Electra proves to be so much like Clytemnestra; she will act in such a way as to continue the train of events. She will do something that in turn will generate a response.

Where, then, does Sophocles intend to leave us with regard to the question of justice? Justice requires accountability, and so causality.[79] Yet, the only straightforward causality to appear in the *Electra* is in the fictional *logoi*—in poetry. In his account of Orestes' "death," the *paidagōgos* presumes to know not only everything that happens, but why it happens. He gets inside the heads of the charioteers. So while, on the one hand, this *Electra* seems much less haunted than the *Libation Bearers* (for example, at 1424), still, how optimistic is it? How bad really are this Aegisthus and Clytemnestra?

The First Stasimon: 473–515

The chorus seem to affirm this apparent optimism. Our first indication that this appearance is deceptive is that the stasimon occurs when it does. In *Antigone* the first stasimon (332–83) gives the guard time to return to the corpse of Polynices to discover Antigone reburying her brother. An artfully ordered plot would place a stasimon, which in one way takes place outside the time-world of the plot, where it provides time for something in that time-world to transpire. Here, however, that seems pointless. Why should an interval be required between the time Chrysothemis leaves for the tomb and the time Clytemnestra emerges from the house? As we saw, this chorus is not actually grounded in the action of the play. No more is the content of this stasimon grounded. The corresponsion in its single strophic system between *tharsos* (boldness or the confidence that inspires boldness) in the strophe (479) and *tharsos* in the antistrophe (495) makes explicit their confidence that justice (476) will prevail.

---

79 In Greek, *aitia* means both cause and responsibility.

From where, then, does this confidence spring? Their answer— the "begetting lord of the Greeks" (484)—is ambiguous. Most likely, they mean Agamemnon.[80] But perhaps they refer to Pelops (502–03) or even Zeus. Whatever the reference, they mean to appeal to a guarantor who will assure that in the end all get what is coming to them. It is because of their belief in this guarantee that they can make prophecy an issue. If they are not a deranged prophet (473), Justice, foreprophet (*promantis*), carrying off just things with the strength of her two hands, will in no great time be among [them] (475–77). And unless this proves true, they contend, prophesy and divine decrees do not exist for mortals (498–500). On the face of it then, they have made this case—the punishment of the murderers of Agamemnon—a test case for prophecy and for justice. If the two do not show themselves here, "never, never" (496) will they do so.

And yet, we have from the outset of the stasimon some reason to be skeptical of this claim to confidence. The strophe begins with the words *ei mē* (unless), as does the last line of the antistrophe—suggesting something like circular motion in the system. Having made the murder of Agamemnon a test case for justice in the antistrophe, in the epode they sum up by immediately addressing Pelops and thereby call our attention to what underlies this test case—the curse on the house of Atreus. Having mentioned Pelops, they might, perhaps should, have traced the curse back to Tantalus, who fed his son, Pelops, to the gods. Instead, they begin the story with what happens to Pelops once he reaches Greece. Oenomaus, king of Pisa (near Olympia), has a prophecy that he will be killed by his son-in-law. Accordingly, he decrees that no one can wed his daughter, Hippodamia, without first having defeated him in a chariot race in which the penalty for losing will be death. His team of horses, a gift from his father, Ares, seems to assure him of victory. After suing for Hippodamia's hand, Pelops bribes Myrtilus, the servant of Oenomaus, to sabotage his master's chariot so that he can win the race and not suffer the fate of all Hippodamia's previous suiters. His victory results in the

---

80   They are addressing Electra. So, they seem to mean the lord of the Greeks who begot "you." Froehlich emends the text by adding you/*se*, which would eliminate the ambiguity (*Sophocles Fabulae*, 79).

death of Oenomaus. After its conclusion Myrtilus attempts to keep Hippodamia for himself. He is killed by Pelops. The chorus seem to trace the curse on the House of Atreus to Pelops's "crime" (509–15). But what exactly is the crime here? Yes, Pelops killed Oenomaus, but how else was he to free Hippodamia from her father? Yes, he killed Myrtilus, but Myrtilus reneged on his agreement and tried to keep Hippodamia for himself. It does look, then, as though the very attempt of the chorus to bring a kind of closure to the story, contrary to their intent, highlights its lack of closure. One cannot escape the circularity of action exemplified by the stasimon. The chorus proclaim their confidence that in the end Justice will prevail and strike down the evildoers, but there is no end. Their very confidence is based on the never-ending character of this process; the punishment, the "brazen clawed fury," seems almost mechanical in its nature. Is the dream alone, then, the source of their confidence (480–81)? But since they never offer an interpretation of it, it would have to be not the content, but the *fact* of the dream. That Clytemnestra dreams means that she cannot forget. Her punishment is her guilt, and so the fact of her crime is in some way her punishment.

The first stasimon paves the way for the following problem to emerge in Electra's conversation with her mother. That conversation will highlight the tension between justice and shame grounded in piety. The prosecution of justice requires making its violation, crime, visible. Someone does something bad. We want to *enact* punishment on them, to *do* something bad to them, and so "make the punishment fit the crime." Yet the goal is not really the enacting; we do not really so much want to do something to them as to cause them to suffer. The goal is not to even things out in some cosmic order—some cosmic scheme of action and reaction. It is rather that we want the person doing the bad thing to suffer in the same way by very virtue of his action that the other whom he treated badly suffered. It is a sort of perverse version of the golden rule—do unto others so that they suffer as they have caused others to suffer. We want the punishment not to fit the crime, but to be the crime. Procne kills her children to punish her husband and suffers as a result. Electra, then, does not so much care about Clytemnestra's death (she always seems to refer to it by way of euphemisms); it is Clytemnestra's suffering as she has suffered that is important.

This brings us to the question of shame. One can feel shame at what
one has done without anything external happening at all. This happens
when we somehow acknowledge that our shameful/*aischron* action
(which is internal) is ugly/*aischron* (external). Electra wants Clytemnestra to be ashamed. This has to do with a curious feature of the play we
have previously noted—that the thousand or so lines in which Electra is
central could be altogether removed, and with respect to what happens,
the action, nothing would change. And yet it is Electra, for whom the
play is named, in whom we are most interested. Now, Orestes is utterly
dispassionate about killing his mother, and his stated goal for killing
Aegisthus and Clytemnestra is to get his property back—it is the most
superficial of possible goals for him. Orestes stays on the surface. He
deals with the visible, the external, what can be understood in terms of
justice.[81] One might say that for Orestes matricide is really nothing but
murder—there is no depth to his action. A person was killed. The score
must be evened—a death for a death. We see him kill neither Clytemnestra nor Aegisthus. In fact, the play ends before we can be certain that
Aegisthus dies. All of this suggests that the real "action" of the play is
Electra's. And for her, the question is never Clytemnestra's death. She
is more upset about the adultery; this is the cause of her dire suffering.
Electra wants to even things up by making Clytemnestra feel as she has
felt the suffering she has caused. In her conversation with her mother
our attention is repeatedly drawn to how similar the two are. In Greek
tragedy we are supposed to get an imitation of action, but we seem only
to get speeches, *logoi*.[82] This is because true action is not what happens
outside, but about what happens inside. So-called "action movies," while
often entertaining, are ordinarily also superficial. They have no depth
because they are about what happens outside.

"Going inside" is connected to the question of piety. In order to show
his sincerity, to display his inner motive, the *paidagōgos* is told to lie about
his death and then swear an oath to the truth of what he has said (47–48),
but he doesn't do that.[83] Instead, he gives an elaborate account of what

81   See page 64 above.
82   Aristotle, *On Poetics*, Chapter 6.
83   See pages 60–61 above.

happened externally. To make Orestes' death believable, he makes it "visible" in speech. He narrates the plot of an action movie. The gods by whom we swear are akin to this process. They are signs of our need to externalize the internal. They "see" what goes on inside us as though it were available to sight and punish us accordingly. This punishment is intended to reach inside us and make us ashamed of our injustice. We need the gods to make this whole system of justice work. Aeschylus had seen that justice as vengeance (something internal, to be sure, but human) had to be replaced. In its stead he posited a justice grounded in equality under the law, treating each citizen as a human being capable of guilt. Justice externalizes this as legal guilt. At the same time, Aeschylus realizes that simply replacing inner guilt—the furies—is insufficient, for then those declared guilty and punished would feel only pain, but not guilt. In his *Electra*, Sophocles focuses on the fact that action is not action (it is somehow only motion) without this inner component. This, in turn, is connected to the issue of matricide. Why does Orestes feel no guilt for killing his mother? Thinking it just and justifying it as though it were simply a matter of law, he unduly externalizes his action. Sophocles thus writes a play to highlight what, as ever only implicitly present in our lives as well as in the *Libation Bearers*, can easily be lost sight of. Matricide is not really a legal issue. It is rather a case in which you kill what you were once "with," once identical to.[84] This seems better understood as inducing shame than being unjust. When you take something from your little sister, it may well be unfair, but the reproach you hear is more likely to be, "You should be ashamed of yourself," than "You were unjust." Orestes' killing of Clytemnestra ought, in its way, to be its *own* punishment because, while it is an attack on her for having killed his *own* (i.e., Agamemnon as his father), it is experienced as an attack on him*self*—i.e., on the being with whom he was once identical. In a less tragic, more general, sense one might say this is simply growing up. You need to affirm your independent identity (your self) and can do so only by separating yourself from your parents—especially from your

---

84 To be with in Greek is *suneinai*. It has various senses of to associate or have intercourse with, or be in the presence of (one of which is to be with a teacher, or even attend a lecture). As in English, it can also mean to have sexual intercourse.

mother with whom you were once one. In defense of yourself, you utter interesting self-contradictions like "I wish you were not my mother." Growing up, then, means being ashamed of yourself in your affirmation of yourself. Adam and Eve grow up when they learn of good and evil, become like God, and must leave the Garden of Eden. The peculiarity of Sophocles' *Electra* is its separation of growing up into its elements— each somehow purified. Orestes does the deed—completes the separation—but feels no shame. Electra suffers shame for not doing the deed; she suffers for having remained in the house. We experience the play and find ourselves wanting him to suffer and her to act. And yet this reaction suggests that the action is on the one hand wrong and on the other right.

Tragedy is always an external display of the impossibility of externalizing the internal. It is the external, visible, beautiful, and noble display of the internal, invisible, ugly, and shameful. And so, the subject of tragedy generally is really Hades, the invisible (*a-eides*) place, that must and cannot be a place. We require visible, external institutions like tragedy to prevent us from being overly confident in our sense of justice, to righteously temper our self-righteousness, to keep us from being Orestes and at the same time to force us to externalize, to depersonalize our anger, to keep us from being Electra.

The Second Episode: 516–822

The second episode starts with Clytemnestra defending herself for having killed Agamemnon (516–51). It generates a conversation with Electra in which the question of shame is particularly prominent.[85]

---

85   Greek uses several words for shame or shameful. Together, three of them, *aidōs*, *aischunē*, and *aischron*, occur thirteen times in the *Electra* (at lines 254, 486, 518, 559, 586, 593, 615, 616, 621—twice, 989—twice, and 1083). Electra is on stage for all of them, Orestes for none. Eight of the instances of *aidōs*, *aischunē*, and *aischron* occur in the second episode, in the conversation between Electra and her mother. After line 1083, when the part of the play that belongs to Orestes begins, the part in which the actual act of killing Clytemnestra and Aegisthus takes over the plot, the question of shame simply disappears.

Clytemnestra's initial defense has several interesting difficulties. Its first word is a form of the verb *aniēmi*. It usually means something like "to send up," "produce" or "give rise to," which gives rise to "to let go," and then "to let loose" or "to set free." Herodotus uses it in Book 2 of his *History* to refer to animals who, as held to be sacred, are allowed to range at large.[86] Does Clytemnestra unwittingly liken Electra's roaming when Aegisthus is away from home with that of sacred animals? She defends herself for the murder of Agamemnon by charging him with the murder of "your sister (or your same-blood—*tēn sēn homaimon*, 531). Why, when it would be so appropriate here, does she fail to name Iphigenia, or indeed anywhere in the play? She says that Electra is outspoken in her criticism of her mother as over-bold (but perhaps just bold—*tharseia*,) and as ruling beyond what is just (521). Does she mean excessively just or just beyond measure? The language of the two charges admits of almost opposite interpretations. Clytemnestra claims to have acted with justice (528), a claim that seems to depend on another—i.e., that Iphigenia belonged to her and not to Agamemnon, for the pain of her labor in childbearing exceeded by far his labor in sowing the seeds (532–33). She is in the right because Agamemnon took her own from her—she does not acknowledge Iphigenia to have been a joint project. In all these ways, her initial argument raises as many questions as it answers. Even so, Clytemnestra has a rather strong case. Did the Argives demand the sacrifice of Iphigenia, or even approve of it (534–36)? If Agamemnon waged the war for the sake of his brother, Menelaus, then why not sacrifice one of the two children of Menelaus and Helen rather than Iphigenia (536–42)? Helen, and not Clytemnestra, after all, was the cause of the war.

Electra's reply (552–608) begins unexpectedly politely. She asks that her mother permit her to speak on behalf of the murdered man and her sister. She then calls father-killing most shameful (558–59), but of course Clytemnestra's crime is not patricide—she killed her husband, not her father. We begin to see that Electra sees the deed only as she suffered it. She does not, indeed seems to be unable to look at the deed through Clytemnestra's eyes. Is killing a husband more shameful than

86 2.65.

killing a child? And while Electra will claim that the killing of Agamemnon was unjust, she prefaces this claim by saying that with an act of this kind, it really doesn't matter whether it was just or unjust. Her argument for the injustice of the killing rests on the fact that Artemis told Agamemnon to do what he did. Artemis was angry with him. Electra first urges Clytemnestra to ask the goddess why she was angry, but then quickly adds that since it would not be *themis*—divinely just—to question a god, Electra will tell her (565). And yet this forces us to ask how it is that Electra knows. She gets the story she tells—that Agamemnon offended Artemis by boasting after slaying one of her deer—by hearsay (566). As it is not *themis* to ask for explanations from the gods, unless they tell us, we know their intentions only second-hand by way of interpretation—something like prophecy is necessary. Yet, even if one should accept the account Electra has heard, since Agamemnon is being punished for boasting, wouldn't the need to sacrifice his daughter still be his fault? And even if we accept this punishment, why should Iphigenia suffer? Why couldn't Agamemnon have forfeited his own life? Or, since Artemis punished him by keeping the fleet at Aulis for want of wind so that he could not carry out his expedition against Troy, couldn't he have called the war off? If Artemis did not relent, the Greeks might have marched home by land. Electra gives a putatively causal account that means to show that Agamemnon had no options other than the one he took, but that doesn't seem to be true. Halfway through her speech she warns Clytemnestra that if it is legitimate to take Agamemnon's life in recompense for Iphigenia's, Clytemnestra's life is equally forfeit for the killing of her husband. She neglects to push the argument one step further to ask about the fates of herself and her brother.

Perhaps the most important feature of Electra's charge is that she identifies as most shameful that Clytemnestra sleeps with Aegisthus and has children with him (586–88). But previously father-killing had been most shameful (559). Are the two crimes somehow the same? If Clytemnestra had not gone on to sleep with Aegisthus, would this, in some way, have diminished her guilt in Electra's eyes? Does Clytemnestra somehow dilute the principle that moved her to avenge Iphigenia by creating a new (as far as we know, wholly hypothetical) set of offspring? Electra ends her speech by challenging her mother to call her shameless, saying that if she is by nature skillful in such deeds, she comes by this shamelessness honestly by way of her mother. This is meant to be scathingly ironic, but is it? When the chorus speak at 609, saying "I see anger breathing forth, but if it is with justice, I do not yet perceive the thinking behind it," they might be speaking either to Clytemnestra or to Electra.[87] The ambiguity is grounded in another—that, while anger is on the outside, and so visible, justice is hidden within.

The exchange between Clytemnestra and Electra is connected to the circularity of the first stasimon. Both mother and daughter believe them-selves aggrieved, and this blinds them to the similarity of their claims. They are related much as are enemies in war, where each side must work up hatred for the other in order to justify the actions that battle demands of them. Accordingly, Electra depicts her mother's *nature* as simply evil and worthy of hatred and does not really judge her *action*. She seems to say (616–25): "I feel shame (and you can't see it), and I am forced by necessity owing to the hostility that comes from you and your deeds (shameful deeds taught by shameful matters)." Electra assumes her inner core—her shame—is not visible, but she assumes her mother is perfectly transparent. And she assumes this despite the regular ambiguity of Clytemnestra's language. When Clytemnestra responds, "I and my word and my deeds make you speak too much" (621–23), she means to say "I am not only my deeds, I am not even my words, and you are responding in deed by words beyond what you should speak given what you can re-ally know about me." In response, Electra says "But you say it, not I. You make the deeds done, and the deeds find the words" (624–25). For Electra, deeds imply meanings or words, and words reveal the inner core—the self. This seems to be the issue that divides them. Electra as-sumes she knows Clytemnestra through and through, but Clytemnestra does not assume the same of her daughter. Clytemnestra, for example, before praying swears by Artemis, who was the god who punished Agamemnon. She invokes a goddess to attest to her hidden inner intent and says that Electra will not escape from [her own] *tharsos* (with its ambiguity of boldness or courage, or over-boldness or rashness) when Aegisthus returns (626–27). Electra's response to this ambiguity (is her

87 Compare 520-24 with 577-84.

mother threatening punishment for her rashness or lamenting the utterly predictable results of her courage?) is ironic but in a way that is altogether unself-aware. In her anger, assuming she understands that Clytemnestra has been carried off by anger and does not know how to listen (628–29), Electra shows that she does not know how to listen.

Just before the *paidagōgos* reenters, Clytemnestra prays while making sacrificial offerings (of which we hear only now) presumably to a statue of Apollo (637) in front of the house. She bids him listen to her hidden oracular word, a tale (*muthos*) to be unfolded only among friends and not for the *polis* at large (638–42). What does she mean to hide and why? The most obvious possibility is that she is praying for the death of Orestes. This might account for her gullible response to the story the *paidagōgos* will soon relate of the death of her son (Aegisthus will want to see the body). The death of Orestes would quite literally then be the answer to her prayers, for it would mean that she will not have to kill him, and he will not be able to kill her. But if this is what Clytemnestra is hiding, what are we to make of what she calls her "double dreams" (645)? This is the account given by Chrysothemis of the dream of which Clytemnestra speaks:

> There is a *logos* that she looked at a father,
> of you and of me, for a second intercourse
> coming back into the light. Then, to fix it in the hearth
> he took hold of a scepter he himself once used to bear,
> and now Aegisthus [bears]. And from this
> grew up a teeming shoot, which
> came to overshadow all the Mycenaean land.
>   (417–23)

Now the obvious reading of this account of the dream (which is a third-hand account) is that the offshoot of the scepter is Orestes. This would mean he is a great danger to Clytemnestra. His overshadowing the whole land foretells her demise. And yet, might not the second intercourse of Clytemnestra with Agamemnon mean an intercourse, a companionship with a second Agamemnon, a new Agamemnon, who will live with her? Could this be Orestes? The dream, a double dream, seems then to have two readings. One suggests Orestes will kill his mother. The second suggests the possibility of a second "marriage." Orestes will live with Clytemnestra and share rule with her. This reference to the double dream comes directly after Electra has indicated that her mother's most serious crime is not the murder but her adultery. Now, that Clytemnestra may not be perfectly satisfied with her situation seems indicated at 660–61, where Sophocles has the *paidagōgos* ask if he has come to the house of Aegisthus. Perhaps Clytemnestra thought she needed Aegisthus to rule with her only until another could take his place, until Orestes grew to manhood, and so, perhaps she toys with the possibility, should Orestes be willing, of a reconciliation where Aegisthus would be "removed" and replaced on the throne by her son. Is this another version of what she may only say secretly? This, then, would be the meaning of her plea to Apollo to fulfill the double dream, and would be her way out of the difficulty Orestes' "death" confronts her with—i.e., whether to rejoice or weep (766–68). This is not the obvious meaning of her words; it is only the possible meaning. We are obviously not done with the discrepancy between speech and meaning built into *logos*.

At line 660 the *paidagōgos* arrives to announce the death of Orestes. Clytemnestra's reaction is, as we have already seen, complicated. Her grief is not so utter as Electra's, but neither does she simply rejoice. The announcement, the long story invented by the *paidagōgos*, is also complicated. Orestes had told him to swear by the gods to the truth of his message; this story is his substitute for a false oath. An account of what is "visible" and outside replaces what is unavailable and inside.[88] In this external account the "dead" Orestes is presented as a man whose external nature so perfectly reflected his internal powers that to no one's surprise he carried off prizes in all the events at the Delphic games. This, of

88 Compare this with *Agamemnon* 264–350, where Clytemnestra enters to announce to the chorus the fall of Troy. When they ask for proof, she tells them of an elaborate system of signal fires that she and Agamemnon had established (281–316) prior to his departure. Her account is altogether plausible, but the chorus do not readily believe her. Only when she adds a long poetic account describing the suffering of the Trojans (320–47) do they believe her and praise her and say she speaks "prudently like a man of good sense" (351).

course, is the power of fiction, of poetry, where the poet makes alto-gether manifest in the hero's "looks" that he is a hero (686–87). In the real world, however, looks are deceiving; we cannot be certain who will win the prize until the race is run. That's what makes horse races. Despite his initial claim about Orestes, even the *paidagōgos* must acknowledge this (690)—we work backwards from the outcome. By the end of the *paidagōgos*'s story, we see one cannot really expect theodicy to be so obvious, for Orestes, with the best nature of all, is killed. At the begin-ning, then, the *paidagōgos* seems to claim that "God's in his heaven, and all's right with the world," but by the end of his story he describes Orestes' death as the greatest of all evils he has seen (763).

The *paidagōgos* begins his account of the final event, the chariot race in which Orestes dies, with various preliminary details and the start of the race (698–719). This is followed by an account of a multi-car crash and pile-up of chariots (723–33), from which we are told Orestes and the Athenian charioteer wisely hold back (731–41). At 742–56 (lines 720–22 need to be inserted following line 740[89]), Orestes makes his move and crashes. He dies and is burned on a funeral pyre (757–60). The account ends with the *paidagōgos* claiming to have reported cor-rectly and to have seen all of this himself (761–73). There are ten char-ioteers in the race—an Achaean, a Spartan, two Libyans, Orestes, an Aetolian, a Magnesian, an Aenian, an Athenian, and a Boeotian. They are Greeks from all over, including Greek colonies in North Africa and Thessaly. Argos, Orestes' city, is more or less geographically in the cen-ter of the places represented. The crucial thing about the race itself is that two chariots emerge after the crash because their charioteers, Orestes and the Athenian, compete by doing nothing. The Athenian sim-ply stops, and Orestes holds back. We see from lines 720–22 that it is because Orestes takes a chance and becomes active, because he tries to move ahead of the Athenian by cutting too close to the turning stele, that he hits it, his axle breaks, he crashes, goes head over heels, and dies. In the end, then, the most passive of the participants wins. Orestes loses a

---

89 Piccolomini seems right to move the lines. They interrupt the account of the crash, and don't really make sense where they are, whereas after line 740 they account for what happens to Orestes.

contest of passivity by acting. The *paidagōgos* has given a paean to non-action, a paean that is in fact a celebration of a non-event, and it is given in such a form as extra-dramatically to please the passive Athenian spectators in the audience who watch their fellow Athenian win.[90]

The story seems to place Clytemnestra deeply at odds with herself. Fate has removed her from an impossible situation. So, she is relieved and grateful; yet her sadness seems genuine. Clytemnestra indicates that for her as mother, hatred of a child is not possible. Electra, on the other hand, finds Clytemnestra's response altogether hateful. We return, then, to the question of the meaning of matricide, and so of motherhood. The mother may find her daughter unjust, but there remains a distinction between recognizing injustice and hatred. For Clytemnestra, Electra is wrong, but does not thereby deserve total elimination. Matricide, "killing the mother," means the removal of a constraint that prevents us from killing those who get in the way of "right." Here, Clytemnestra represents the enemy soldier whom one has to get past thinking of as a human being. The elimination of Clytemnestra means removing the possibility of treating an obstacle as altogether anonymous without going through the level of pure hatred. Electra must become convinced that her mother is the embodiment of pure evil, and that she therefore could not have been the agent of justice. Accordingly, to Electra, Clytemnestra's ambivalence must seem fraudulent. She must believe Clytemnestra would have killed Agamemnon for the sake of Aegisthus even had Iphigenia not been sacrificed. And so, adultery must be Clytemnestra's real crime.

Had Electra put the report of the *paidagōgos* alongside what Chrysothemis reports from Agamemnon's tomb, had she compared the two in terms of the evidence they offer, it is not clear why she would favor the former. The report of the *paidagōgos* is based on what he putatively saw, but Chrysothemis also speaks of what she saw. Electra ought to have put them side by side to compare them, but she doesn't, can't really. We don't experience things in this way. *Pathos*, experience, always comes in a sequence of experiences. And our experience is conditioned, not simply by what causes it, but by what precedes it and sets

90 This play is being performed in the theater of Dionysus on the side of the Acropolis in Athens before an audience of 30,000 Athenians.

the tone for it. When forced to acknowledge herself as pure suffering, as purely passive, Electra says, "I am one who knows this too, one who knows above all and too much, [I] with a life of many terrible things (*deinōn*) swept all together through all the months" (850–52). For human beings learning comes through suffering—*pathei mathos.*[91] Knowing, as undergoing, is always somehow temporal. Electra's doubt of the authenticity of Clytemnestra's grief (804–07) allows her to idealize her own grief. She understands the death of Orestes as equivalent to her own death because it has doomed her to utter passivity. As Electra becomes mourning, perfect mourning, she commits a sort of passive suicide.

Kommos *(taking the place of the Second Stasimon): 823–70*

In various ways, Sophocles' *Electra* turns on the question of delay—the delays of Orestes' return to Argos, of the meeting of Orestes and Electra, of Chrysothemis in going to Agamemnon's tomb, of Orestes and Electra at the door of the house and, of course, of the killing of Aegisthus at the end of the play. This has something to do with justice. Cato the censor is said to have claimed that in ancient Rome if you caught your wife in the act of adultery, you were allowed by law to kill her on the spot,[92] but presumably only on the spot and not after some delay. To kill her immediately, "in the heat of passion," suggests that one's motive is pure, and the adultery is not being used as a ruse or ploy. Delay would make the manipulation of the law possible. On this account, true justice operates rather like a stimulus-response relation. Punishment is an immediate consequence of the crime. Now, it is in fact not simply clear that this guarantees justice, for even in an immediate response, the motives of all concerned will remain opaque. The visibility claim makes these actions in question all too mechanistic. Human behavior is never so straightforward. Justice, then, would seem to require not an immediate response, but rather an articulation, a *logos*, of what exactly took place, and this is not possible from one involved in the action. It requires a re-view. For human beings this means detachment in time—a delay to make clear what it is that actually

91 *Agamemnon*, 178; see also 250.
92 Cato is quoted by Aulus Gellius, *Attic Nights* 10.23

transpired and its significance. The problem, again for human beings, is that this delay might also give rise to brooding and resentment, and these obscure rather than clarify things. In the *Electra* the various delays seem to be hothouses for the growth of passion. On the one hand then, justice requires immediate punishment—"this justice should exist directly for all, whoever in any way would act beyond the laws, should die" (1505-6). Passion demands that there be no delay. On the other hand, delay seems to be a necessary condition for the possibility of thinking through what has happened. Justice cannot be automatic and still be just. Time, then, is at once the necessary condition for justice and what makes justice impossible. The problem is bringing Orestes and Electra together in time.

The chorus begin the *kommos* that substitutes for the second stasimon by asking Electra two things—where are Zeus's thunderbolts, and where is the sun? Why are criminals not punished, and why is their criminality not exposed? They lament the absence of justice—of the immediate action it demands and of the awareness it needs that is possible only through delay. Then they ask Electra why she weeps. Since she has always wept, at first this seems a strange question, but the chorus anticipate an important change in Electra as her cries begin to alternate subtly between simple expressions of grief (*e e aiai*, 826; *e e iō*, 840) and a word that may indicate either grief or anger, *pheu* (828, 840). Their response is similarly ambiguous when they tell her not to cry out so loudly (831)—they may be afraid of discovery, or they may be telling her "It's not so bad." But since Electra is her suffering, for her to be consoled would be for her to be undone. Accordingly, she takes their advice to entail her utter destruction (832). When the chorus do not understand, she explains. By holding out hope for those who have manifestly (*phanerōs*, 834) gone to Hades (although it isn't really so *phanerōs*; Orestes' death is only hearsay), the chorus destroy Electra, who is already "melting away," still more. Suffering requires hope. What the chorus offer is not hope for a particular avenger, but blind hope. They offer Electra hope as such, which when disappointed would lead to the epitome of suffering, utter hopelessness—suffering as such. With the best of intentions, they will bring her to the peak of despair.

The chorus introduce the story of Amphiaraus, presumably to restore some hope to Electra. Amphiaraus had the gift of prophecy and so knew

he would perish when Oedipus's son Polyneices attacked Thebes, to regain the kingship from his brother, Eteocles. Amphiaraus hid so that he
would not have to go. Bribed with a golden necklace, Eriphyle, his wife,
betrayed him to Polyneices, after which Amphiaraus told his son, Alk-
maeon, to kill Eriphyle if Amphiaraus should die at Thebes.[93] Here the
crucial element of the story is that Amphiaraus retains his soul in Hades.
It is the revenge exacted from beneath the earth that seems to move Electra back from *e e aiai* to *pheu*, to an angry exclamation of grief and then
to the decision to exact punishment, to act, herself. Yet the conclusion
Electra draws is that her fate is akin to that of Amphiaraus in Hades with
a soul, and akin as well to that of Agamemnon if he has a soul. For Electra, presumably because one is so detached from this world, to be in
Hades is to be in a position to know (even "hyper-know"), but because
of this very detachment, those in Hades are unable to act. And so, to be
able really to know means to be without alternatives—simply to take
whatever hits you. When we fully recognize the nature of what is, we
see its necessity. As suffering knowledge, we cannot act; and, as suffering, we can only despair. When Electra announces this relation between
knowledge and suffering (850-52), her version of *pathei mathos*, the
chorus immediately respond with "We know, you were —lamenting."
Or perhaps, "We are detached, you were suffering." Now, their response
could also be read "we know that you were lamenting," but even then,
they make a distinction between knowing and suffering, while, according to Electra, they must in some way suffer in knowing. Only because
they are the almost totally indeterminate chorus, with no apparent reason
for being in the play, can they proceed as though this were not true. This
chorus is not really a person. And so, when the chorus say of the violent
death of Orestes, "unviewable is the mutilation" (866), on the one hand
they mean it is horrible, but on the other, they do mean it is unviewable,
invisible, to them, for they have no vested interest in it. Electra confirms
this problem of invisibility when she immediately responds that Orestes,
as a foreigner, was covered up without her hands and so without a proper

93 For pieces of this traditional story (but not all of it) see Homer's *Odyssey*,
     15.243; Hesiod's *Catalogues of Women*, 99; Aeschylus's *Seven Against
     Thebes,* 456 and 712, and Euripides' *Suppliants*, 158.

funeral or mourners (865–70). Now, this "invisibility" means that Electra has not actually experienced the death of her brother. Since she understands knowledge to be experience, undergoing, this should move her to recognize that she does not really know Orestes to be dead, and so it should prepare her to be open for what she is about to hear from Chrysothemis. Yet it doesn't. *Pathei mathos* means learning through experience, but also learning through suffering. The two are not accidentally linked, for to experience means to move through our worlds and run into things. What resists this movement is what we know—"the truth hurts." Accordingly, we are more inclined to believe things that unsettle us. Pain seems more real than pleasure. Nightmares move us more than daydreams, and so are more likely to demand interpretation. And, of course, there is the issue of time. What strikes us first has pride of place; it has the stamp of reality. And so, for Electra, Orestes' death is real.

The Third Episode—Electra and Chrysothemis: 871–1057

We have just been told that knowing is suffering or experiencing. When Chrysothemis enters, twice claiming to bring pleasure (871 and 873) to her sister, she has raised the question of the relation of knowledge to pleasure and pain. When Electra doubts this is now possible, and Chrysothemis blurts out her news, "Orestes is among us; know this from hearing me, just as you look upon me." (877–78), she brings to the fore another central issue. Electra, who has heard of Orestes' death from the *paidagōgos*, now hears he is alive from her sister. In both instances the question is the reliability of hearsay. And by claiming her tale is as sure as it is sure that Electra now sees her, Chrysothemis raises the question of the relation between knowledge, sight, and hearing.[94] Electra calls her sister mad (879). Apparently, the coincidence of pleasure and knowledge is madness. Electra assumes her sister must have heard a report, a *logos*, from someone (as, of course, she herself has), but Chrysothemis tells her that her *logos* is based on what she has seen. So, we have three levels of knowledge claims: seeing what is manifestly present—

94 It is a common-place that in terms of knowledge sight : hearing :: Athens: Jerusalem.

Chrysothemis's experience; hearing a *logos* based on seeing—from an
eyewitness, i.e., listening either to the *paidagōgos* or to Chrysothemis;
and hearing a *logos* based on a *logos*—hearsay (of course, *paidagōgos*'s
direct experience is fraudulent, and Chrysothemis's experience is in its
way not really direct, since it requires the interpretation of signs—she
reads the scene at the tomb). Accordingly, when Electra replies to her
sister's claim to first-hand experience by asking, "Having what proof
(*pistis*, trust), wretched one?" (887), she really calls into question
whether what we call knowledge does not ultimately rest on trust. The
problem is confirmed when Chrysothemis replies, "Hear, by the gods
(or perhaps, 'by seeing'), so that, learning the rest from me, you may
say whether I am sensible or dull." (889–90). She either invokes the
gods, or on the less likely reading seeing, but either is invoked as an authority. The account itself, and even the experience underlying it, are not
sufficient to generate trust.

   To provide this trust, this proof, Chrysothemis gives a "causal" argument. We have an event: she saw milk, flowers, and newly cut hair
left at Agamemnon's tomb (894–901). Where did it come from, what
was its cause? Chrysothemis did not do it (910); nor was it Electra—
she is not permitted to go outside (911–12); it was certainly not
Clytemnestra, and in any case, she couldn't have done it without their
knowing (913–14). And no one else would care enough to do it. So, by
eliminating all other possibilities, she proves that it had to be Orestes
(915). Now, while indeed this proves to be the case, the argument for it
is not particularly persuasive. Electra is frequently outside (during this
conversation for example), we have heard nothing more of the once
mentioned Iphianassa, and Electra will quickly offer a plausible hypoth-
esis that someone placed these things on the tomb as a memorial for the
dead Orestes (932–33).[95] Still, Chrysothemis draws the interesting conclusion that the same fate does not always attend the same person (916–
17). If Electra is really utterly a sufferer, and so altogether passive, then,
while she is at the mercy of whatever hits her at any time, she might also
be hit by good things. Furthermore, even this good suffering would be

---

95   This is strangely at odds with the claim she is about to make that she and
     Chrysothemis have no friends present to aid them (949).

altogether beyond our control, and so experienced as accidental, and so not meaningful. But the chorus take this very fact to mean that, since we experience things as uncaused, change is always possible. And this, which is in a way simply another angle on the necessary presence of hope within all suffering, means that there can be no pure suffering.

We recognize Electra here. She has turned suffering as undergoing or experiencing, which, in turn, involves being subject to fate, which is experienced as the accidental, into suffering as being pained. And finally, her reason for this transformation is that being a pure sufferer—as passivity means not being an agent, not free—is to be a slave.[96] This leads to the great change in Electra, her decision to act whether with or without the help of Chrysothemis. The movement of the play thus far is designed to make us experience the world through the eyes of Electra, through her paradigmatic passivity. We have been seduced into accepting a sequence of events that is far from necessary. We have been won over to Electra's point of view even though, perhaps because we know, that she is being toyed with. We need to become like Electra so that we think the answer obvious to the question, "What else could she do?" We think we have experienced the total detachment of suffering from action that seems necessary to imagine the possibility of pure action. And at the very moment that we come to be convinced by her suffering, she changes her mind—she will be a cause.

But what sort of cause? After Chrysothemis recounts her experience at the tomb, Electra responds that she pities her sister for her *anoia*, her folly, more literally her mindlessness (920).[97] When Electra says they should do something to lighten their pains, and Chrysothemis suggests sardonically that perhaps they should raise the dead (i.e., a tacit comparison with the apparently quite serious attempt to raise Agamemnon from the dead in the *Libation Bearers*), Electra replies, "It is not what I said. I have not grown senseless (*aphrōn*—without mind, will, or heart)"

96 See 814–16.
97 The relation of the immediacy of mind, knowing, and having seen with the mediacy of hearing and hearsay as erring, and how both are related to pleasure and pain receives considerable stress. In addition to 920, see 921 922, 923 (three times), 925, 926, 927.

(941). When she goes on to urge her sister to see that it will be difficult (945), Chrysothemis responds, "I see" (946). Then she begins relating her intention to kill Aegisthus with the imperative "Hear" (947). Electra has deliberated about this plan (947), warns that Aegisthus is a man who is not so much without deliberation as to allow them to bear children (964). She then itemizes the rewards that will come from following what she has deliberated on (967). Directly after her speech the chorus will characterize all of this as forethought (990), and so emphasize the temporal character of deliberation. During this time while emphasizing her own thoughtfulness, Electra gradually changes the way she speaks of herself and her sister. When quoting what the townsmen will say of them, she repeatedly refers to the two of them in the dual number—they are a pair. At 977, she calls them *kasignētō*, the masculine dual for "sibling." They have become a pair of brothers. She then twice uses the dual relative pronoun *hō* (who or what—978–79), which may be either masculine or neuter. And finally, Electra claims that the people assembled in the *polis* will love and revere them (*toutō, tōde* 981), and honor them (*tōd'* 982) as a masculine pair for their *andreia*—their courage or manliness (982). She sums up by saying that such things will be said of *nō* (984), which is either the dual for "us" or the dual for "mind." Is there a connection between Electra's emphasis on mind as governing her intentions and her progressive masculinizing of herself and her sister?

That Chrysothemis sees a connection seems clear from her remark to the chorus. She begins her refusal to help Electra with "Indeed even before speaking aloud, women, she herself, if she had happened upon the sensible and not the bad would have preserved discretion, just as she has not preserved it." (992–94) "Women," while in the vocative, and so addressing the chorus, is also evocative, reminding us of what Electra has just done to the female. Chrysothemis calls what Electra named *andreia* rather a lack of caution. It is *thrasos*, boldness or rashness (995), and indicates that Electra does not understand what it means to be "by nature a woman and not a man" (997). In the end Chrysothemis urges her sister to restrain her anger (*orgēn*, 1011) so that in time she may acquire mind (*noun*, 1013). There is on the surface a disagreement here about what it means to have mind, to be sensible. For Chrysothemis it means neutralizing present passion so that we may learn over time from past suffering.

It means passively facing our passions, and it is feminine. For Electra it means overcoming passivity so as to become an agent. And it is masculine. Ignoring the chorus's support for Chrysothemis (for them mind is practical, and nothing brings more gain to human beings than being mindful in advance, *pronoia*, and a wise mind, *nous sophos*—1015–16), Electra announces that she will act on her own (1017–20). Her sister replies that had she done that immediately after the killing of Agamemnon, she could have accomplished anything. On the one hand then, Chrysothemis urges Electra to step back, to be more deliberate, and not to rush into an action that will almost certainly fail. On the other hand, she rebukes her for not having acted immediately when the conditions were perfect to do so. Electra is to combine immediacy and detachment. That Chrysothemis unwittingly articulates a judgment about the tension necessarily present within justice in time, leads Electra to react immediately by saying that at the time of Agamemnon's death, by nature she had less mind (1023). We acquire mind, then, over time, by experience—*pathei mathos*. Chrysothemis counters by charging Electra to practice so as to maintain mind throughout life. Electra should strive, then, to make mind atemporal. Electra defends herself by saying "Because you will not act with me, you admonish (*noutheteis*) me in this way," (1025). *Nou-theteis* is literally "you put mind in." In English we tell children to mind us. Here, Electra suggests that it is owing to her guilt that Chrysothemis exhorts her sister to practice minding. Her admonition is not the product of detached mind at all but rather grounded in passion. Accordingly, Electra admires her mind, but hates her for her cowardice (1027). Justice requires mind. It requires the long view, the detached view. However, even if possible, this is problematic for, while it may be in the service of objectivity, it may also provide an excuse for side-stepping the just for the sake of what is immediately useful. Still, justice is not really possible without it. When we appeal to the just, we must invoke a pattern of right[98]—an atemporal justice as one might "experience" it from the point of view of eternity. Electra needs this atemporal justice, she needs mind, *nous*, but at the same time, she can let it become neither mere calculation in the name of some practical goal nor devoid of experience (1041–43).

98 See page 71 above.

Even for Chrysothemis, however, there is a limit to being sensible. She promises her silence twice (1011, 1041) about what Electra plans to do, and both times the ground of her promise is kinship. The principle is not so different from what Clytemnestra had said earlier, "Giving birth is *deinos*, for not even by suffering badly is hatred produced for those one bears." (770–71). This principle is what Electra cannot afford to acknowledge, and what in the end makes it possible for her to contemplate matricide. It is the "mother principle" that places a limit on righteous indignation and on justice understood on the basis of the pattern of right. It is what makes us smile, but still understand and approve of, phrases like "a face only a mother could love." It is what keeps us from condemning a mother who wails in grief after her child has been convicted of a heinous crime. Oddly, it is this principle that grounds Electra's rejection of Chrysothemis's "mind" as too detached, insufficiently invested and passive, and Chrysothemis's rejection of Electra's proposed course of action as too daring, manly, and insufficiently feminine.

Yet, it is difficult to understand how to mix male and female together in the proper proportion. When Chrysothemis attempts to dissuade Electra from her plan to avenge their father, Electra replies that she decided what to do long ago (1049). Apparently her suffering has taken the form of hypothetical action—"If this should happen, then I would do this," or "If Orestes does not come, what would I do? Alas, I would have to do it myself." Accordingly, when Chrysothemis gives up and proposes to leave saying, "For you do not dare to praise my words, nor I your ways." (1050–51), she proposes a distinction not as clear as she thinks it is since words are hypothetical "ways." Drama is an imitation of action. And Electra too contradicts herself, for her contempt for Chrysothemis's sensible pragmatism is at odds with her understanding of the *anoia*—lack of mind—of following Chrysothemis's advice (1053–54). One cannot speak of justice or right without invoking the long view—the pattern of right—and so there is no experience of justice at all apart from its atemporality. When we feel we have been done an injustice and wish to redress the imbalance, we must think we are taking the objective view, that we have right on our side.[99] This very atemporality, however, always threatens to turn justice

99   And so, Kant can claim "Der kategorische Imperativ ist also ein einziger,

into something like calculation, and so, to undermine the experience of it—its attendant passion or suffering.

The Third Stasimon: 1058–97

The third stasimon is puzzling. Why is it there at all? Why do we need it dramatically? It is not clear exactly what it means or how it is meant to comment either on what precedes it or what follows it. The stasimon doesn't really fit in the play in which so many things are intentionally ill-fitting and in which the nature of not fitting is thematic. But why should this be emphasized at precisely this point in the play? Why is it fitting that the stasimon that does not fit, fits in here?

The puzzles do not stop here. The chorus begin the first strophe (1058–69) with a powerful image, presumably meant to apply to Electra and Orestes, of birds "caring for the nourishment of those from whom they sprouted and from whom they found profit" (1060–61).[100] But do birds really do this? Most birds seem not even to recognize their parents after about a year. And if they do not, what does it mean to use this image that does not really exist as a model for behavior? And even if what the chorus say here about birds were true, would it not apply as much to Clytemnestra as to Agamemnon? The chorus then call on the "lightning of Zeus," and thereafter "Uranian divine right" (1063–64)—they mention neither Kronos nor his pun-kin *chronos*. Is this omission meant to remind us that the gods, too, do not do what the birds "do"? They do not nourish their parents. Is Kronos obtrusively omitted to call attention to the fact that he was overthrown by his son and castrated his father? Zeus is invoked for his lightning bolt—his instrument of punishment, which seems to point to particular cases, while Ouranos is called upon as a

---

und zwar dieser: *handle nur nach derjenigen Maxime, durch die du zugleich wollen kannst, dass sie ein allgemeines Gesetz werde.*" Grundlegung zur Metaphysik der Sitten (Hamburg: Felix Meiner Verlag, 1965), 42.

100 Aristotle (*History of Animals* 9.13.2) says this is "chattered about" storks and sometimes bee-eaters, and so he seems to think it is something of an old wives' tale. Modern sources bear him out (The Cornell Lab of Ornithology, https://www.allaboutbirds.org/news/do-young-birds-recognize-their-parents-after-theyve-grown-up/).

generic principle of divine right. Once again, we are called upon to ask what the connection is between the two—between the experience of justice and the pattern of justice. Is the "answer" the problematic missing Kronos/chronos—i.e., time? Once the chorus take the cosmic view, the pattern of justice, the question of justice in this particular case becomes blurred. The non-behavior of birds aloft justifies both the punishment and the defense of Clytemnestra. When the appeal to the Atreidae below (1068), they might mean only the sons of Atreus, and so since Menelaus is still alive, only Agamemnon, but as the word is plural, they seem to mean the whole family, even those who lived prior to Atreus. But, of course, this includes not only Atreus's brother and rival, Thyestes, but also Pelops and Tantalus, the one cut into pieces by the other and fed to the gods. As the appeal to those below involves competing interests, it is not at all clear how it would be received.

If the intent of the first strophe is unclear, that of its antistrophe is notoriously so. The "double din of battle from the children" (1071–72) seems at first to refer to Electra and Chrysothemis (since Orestes is thought to be dead), but might it not also refer to Atreus and Thyestes? They refer to the ever-grieving nightingale, but how is the story of a mother who fed her child to her husband as punishment for his having raped her sister appropriate here? And what exactly do they mean by the "twin fury" (1080)? If the verb *luein* here means "to bring down" or "undo," "twin fury" would refer to the undoing of Aegisthus and Clytemnestra—their punishment, the experience of right; but if it means "let loose," then it would be the fury of Electra and Chrysothemis—their punishing, the enactment of right. The ambiguity again points to the problem of putting together the twin features of justice—Electra and Orestes. Is the stasimon, then, perhaps obtrusive in its ill fit because, having within it the fundamental dualism of the entire play, there is nothing in particular in the play to which it corresponds?

The chorus begin the second strophe (1082–89) by saying "For, child, child, none of the good would choose, by living badly, nameless, to shame fame." (1082–84). Their addressee remains nameless. Do they speak to two children? And the stasimon is throughout ambiguous about to whom it is referring. Then they offer "in one logos" an explicitly "double praise" (1088) "to the child having been called both wise and best" (1089). Is the wise child the detached child, the one knowing the timeless structure of justice? Is the best child the one who does what needs doing when it needs doing, the one immersed in the temporal experience of justice?

In the antistrophe (1090–98) the chorus express a hope that in the future their addressee will as much have the upper hand and wealth over enemies as now dwelling beneath them. The hope is for justice as an evening out, a tit for tat. This evening out is justified because the addressee, while not faring well in the present, shows a piety toward Zeus. This piety demonstrates a belief in the possible reconciliation of the two aspects of justice in Zeus who is, on the one hand, a cosmic principle and, on the other, an historical actor. This would be the resolution not only of the problem of justice, but at the same time of the gods as at once principles and agents. The stasimon as a whole, then, in its frustrating generality, sets the stage for the Fourth Episode. Orestes, the principle of action, and Electra, the principle of passion, will finally come together on stage. There will have to be some sort of resolution of their apartness.

The Fourth Episode—the Recognition Scene: 1098–1231

Orestes finally arrives on the scene addressing the chorus: "Women, have we both listened to things that are right, and do we go rightly to where we ought?" (1098–99). This could almost be an actor's question—"When do I go on?" It emphasizes that the will of Sophocles and not the necessity of the plot of the *Electra* is the cause of Orestes' entrance.[101] There is something accidental about this entrance and about the recognition scene that follows. Having told Electra that it is wrong to lament her brother, for the urn she holds is "not Orestes, except as having been fashioned by *logos*" (1217), he offers as proof of his identity only his word plus his father's *sphagis*, a seal or signet

---

101 See Aristotle, *On Poetics* 1453b30–35. If Orestes is telling the truth here, that he has been inquiring for a long time for where Aegisthus dwells (1101), there seems to be no reason for him to have arrived at precisely this moment.

ring, that shares the imprecision of logos. There is no comparison of hair or feet—not even a pretense of offering immediate, non-transferable proof.

Electra's long response to Orestes' confirmation of his "death" (1126–70) is curious. In light of her brother's death and Chrysothemis's refusal to help her, she has just resolved to avenge her father and kill Aegisthus on her own. And yet in this speech she seems to be welcoming death, even to be claiming that she is already dead.[102] On the one hand, she comes close to making herself a generic symbol. But a symbol of what? She asks Orestes, "by the gods," swearing for the first time in the play, to let her take the funeral urn "in her hands (1120). She then begins a long speech by addressing the funeral urn she bears "with her hands" as "boy" (1129–30) and goes on to wish she had died before stealing him "with her hands" (1132) to send him off to a strange land to save his life and laments that she was not there to wash his corpse with "loving hands" (1138) so that he had to be tended to "by strangers' hands" (1141). Later Orestes will ask Electra whether Clytemnestra has "laid hands on her," and she will respond that her mother mistreats her "with hands" (1195–96). And at the moment of recognition, she will ask, "Do I hold you in my hands?" (1226). So, Electra handed Orestes over to the *paidagōgos*. She now receives his ashes into her hands. She was not there at his death to wash his body by hand so that the handwashing was done by foreigners. Clytemnestra has shown herself unmotherly by laying hands on her, and Electra embraces Orestes in her hands when she discovers who he is. Handling gives the appearance of immediacy.[103] It seems to be proof of the presence of something. And yet here, this immediacy proves at least ambiguous, perhaps illusory. Orestes is not the urn. The mother, the principle of immediacy, can beat the child.

There is a certain circularity in Electra's account. The boy, Orestes, is in her hands at the outset. He returns to her hands as ashes in a funeral

102 "Of course, while I have been killed by you" (1152) means literally that Electra is already dead, more obviously indicate that by putting her in a position where she must kill Aegisthus, Orestes has guaranteed that she will be caught, and be punished with death.
103 See Aristotle, *De Anima* 2.11.

urn. Then he returns to her again as her living brother, whom she has just called "boy" (1220). This shows how little meaningful is Electra's claim that she recognized Orestes' voice and his aspect or appearance (1285–87). She knew Orestes only as a baby; he was then as little Orestes to her as is the funeral urn now. Electra endows him with certain qualities, but he is essentially unrecognizable to her, and necessarily so. Her "hands to hands" speech with these false identities involves ignoring the importance of the intervening years. For Electra, Orestes is what he is; he is somehow timeless. We get no sense that she understands that he might have changed as a result of what he suffered over time. Electra understands Orestes solely as his soul (1127).

And what about her? She claims that he was never more his mother's object of love than hers, and always called her his nurse (1145–47). She says that Clytemnestra is called a mother but does nothing like a mother (1194) and refers to her as a "non-mother" (1153). Even though he is a now grown man, she addresses him as "boy" (1220—see also 1130 and 1430). The gist of Electra's entire speech is to replace Clytemnestra with herself, and so appropriate Orestes' maternal loyalty. But then she would have sent her "child" away to protect him out of a passion not so different from the passion that moves her mother to avenge Iphigenia, the child she was unable to protect. While Electra becomes mother in more ways than she knows, still the consequence of denying Clytemnestra as mother is to remove whatever hesitation might have been present to kill her.

Insofar as Orestes is affected, he will be affected not by "the mother" but by Electra's motherly affection for him. This is what becomes clear in the remainder of the recognition scene (1171–230). At first Orestes does not actually recognize Electra; he "knows" her only as what she is supposed to be. She is a *logos* for him, a type—an *eidos* (1177). But he has now undergone something (had a *pathos*?) that affects his ability to speak, his *logos*, or reason (1174–75). Electra confirms this change with a pun when, in order to know why he is suddenly *alogos*, without speech, she asks him, "What pain/*algos* did you have?" (1176). Until now, Orestes has stood for speech/*logos* without experience or suffering/*pathos*. Here, he seems to hurt for Electra, and so he laments (1179). The cause of this hurt he believes her to feel is ambiguous. On the one hand, Orestes hurts her unnecessarily by concealing his identity. On the other hand, Electra, in her typically idealizing way, thinks he means to point to Clytemnestra as the cause ("with hands both by indignities and all bad things"—1196). In any case, the formula for Orestes' suffering seems to be, "I am the only one who has come feeling pain with your *kaka*/evils." (1201). It is by second hand experience of Electra's ills—by sym-pathy—that he suffers.

The crucial movement of the first part of the episode is that if justice is to prevail, the plot requires the coming together, not so much of Electra and Orestes, but of what the two represent—particular *pathos* and detached *nous*, mind. When the characters actually meet and recognize each other, in order to act, Orestes must feel through Electra, and so we watch him for the first time feel, suffer. But to act, Electra needed Orestes to be absent—she resolves to act only after he is proclaimed dead. At 1159, she calls him a *morphē*, a shape and a *skia*, the word used for a shade in Hades and, like our shadow, indicating something that is a surface only and has no depth. We have seen from the title, from the number of lines she has, and from her time on the stage that the play is clearly Electra's. Yet the action is completed not by her, but by Orestes. He acquires second-hand passion, second-hand first-hand experience, and proceeds to act. After a long delay, the title character was forced to articulate the need to combine *pathos* and *nous*, seems to do so, resolves to act, but in the end Orestes' presence thwarts the action toward which the whole play has been moving. Why?

We have noticed a series of dualisms in the *Electra*. Suffering or experience—*pathos*—is in tension with mind. Within mind, there is a tension between the more detached *nous* and the less detached and more practical *phrēn*. There is a tension as well between *pathos* as suffering, and action. The two show up as hybrids in Electra and Orestes. Her suffering becomes an action intended to cause Clytemnestra to suffer, and his action proves possible only because of his second-hand participation in Electra's suffering. It is as though he can only be an actor by being a spectator of a drama. The difference between these poles, which are always represented by the two siblings, seems to point to the male/female dichotomy, and then to the difference between mere sequence and cause, and to what occurs in time as opposed to what is atemporal, to the experience of right as opposed to the pattern of right, to acting immediately as opposed to delay, and to sight (being present, being with, immediate hands-on experience, intercourse) as opposed to hearing (being absent, mediated experience, hearsay, poetry). These dualisms show up as well in crucial terms like *dikē* and *Kairos*, terms seeming initially unproblematically one.

The overall problem of the *Electra*, then? The *Libation Bearers* is really Orestes' story. It isn't called *Electra* and, as we saw, there is even some reason to think that it, and not the trilogy, was called the *Oresteia*. Electra disappears from the play half-way through. While at the end Orestes has justified the killing of Clytemnestra and Aegisthus, he is still pursued by inner furies. The play is tragic because Orestes does what he "ought" to do, and nevertheless suffers not despite, but because of what he does. The tragedy of the *Libation Bearers* is thus grounded in a deep contradiction within justice. In Sophocles' *Electra*, Orestes kills Clytemnestra and Aegisthus (although we are not allowed certainty of this last) with Electra's help, yet neither seems to regret their action nor suffer because of it. At first, this seems meant as an expression of a solution to the contradiction within justice. Yet, if so, why is the play tragic? Everything in Sophocles' *Electra* seems to turn on the need to bring *nous* and *pathos* together. On the one hand, if we are to be fair, mind requires that we be cool, detached, clear headed, objective, not involved, not present. We must keep things at a distance. Nothing should be personal. Justice is blind. On the other hand, to be just must we not see clearly, and is seeing not something we do, something for which we must be there? Accordingly, to do anything at all, we must be present, engaged, subjective, passionate, "hot." We must take things in hand. *Pathei mathos*—we learn by suffering. But this necessary suffering needs must cloud our judgment. What makes it possible to judge at all, therefore, makes it impossible to judge perfectly, and short of perfect judgment, our actions must be imperfect. The issue of the *Electra* then? Can there be a suffering undergone by mind that allows it to learn? Is a partially clouded judgment available to us that is adequate to the task of living, and what would such judgment, such a mind, look like? Put differently, how are we to understand, not simply what Orestes and Electra do in *Electra*, but what we do as its audience?

To be a "spectator" of a play, one must be affected by it. As we sit in the audience, we are sym-pathetic. Were we simply pathetic, we would no longer be suffering play as play. It would be altogether real to us. Our perspective would be one with that of the players; it would be not at all atemporal—objective. And yet, were we not to suffer along with the characters, it would be impossible to understand what they are undergoing. On the other side of the coin, actors are at their best when their imitation seems real. And yet, "The most important thing about acting is honesty. If you can fake that, you've got it made."[104] To get anger right, a poet must be extremely observant, detached—a spectator. At the same time, to get anger right, a poet must experience it, and deeply so; he must be an actor.[105] And the same holds for us, the audience of the poet's work. This duplicity is at the heart of *mimēsis*—imitation—and we are by nature mimetic creatures. To be a spectator (*theatēs*) is to look or behold (*theōrein*); it is to be theoretical—to have *nous*. At the same time, to use one's *nous*, one must be moved, have a motion, be emotional. Sophocles' Electra sets itself the task of putting Electra and Orestes together. Justice requires mixing passion and detachment, the result being either dispassionate passion or interested disinterest—hands-on in not taking a hand in. Sophocles may display this mixture as problematic, but he does not mean us to think it simply impossible. He rather shows us that in thinking through Electra, as spectators or contemplators, we exemplify its possibility, however problematic. The problematic togetherness of Electra and Orestes is an imitation of the problematic nature of the spectator of a drama, which is, in turn, an imitation of the problematic nature of human beings—" . . . in the image of God He created it, male and female he created them."[106]

---

104 Used by George Burns in his *The Third Time Around*, but present earlier in a variety of anonymous sources.
105 See Aristotle's *On Poetics*, Chapter 17.
106 This is the theme of the entirety of Aristotle's *On Poetics*. See also, my commentary *The Poetry of Philosophy: on Aristotle's Poetics* (South Bend, IN: St. Augustine's Press, 1999).

Amoibaion *between Electra and Orestes: 1232–87*

An *amoibaion*, a lyric exchange between Electra and Orestes, follows the recognition scene. As the two express their joy, we might expect their song to express something of the meaning of their reunion. Electra begins the strophe (1232–52):

> O births [or, engenderings], births of bodies to me most dear [or, loved], you all came (aorist) just now [or, perfectly], you found out (aorist), were coming back [or, were becoming whole] (imperfect), you saw (aorist) those whom you were in need of (imperfect).
>
> 1232–35

Electra is either using poetic plurals, or she means to refer to Orestes as more than one. Might "engenderings" mean he has undergone a second birth? The mixture of aorists (which point to action at a moment in the past) and imperfects (which point to on-going action in the past) is revealing. By virtue of seeing (aorist) what he needs to see, Orestes has come to be who he really is, and so come to be whole—he has undergone this change in time (hence, the imperfect), but he has somehow done so in a moment (hence, the aorist). What Orestes "was" in general, "was" over no particular time, becomes something more than *logos*, in the moment of being there. Prometheus, forethought, may "know" in advance, in *logos*, what will happen to him if he steals fire from heaven and gives it to human beings, but he does not really know until he experiences his liver daily being eaten by an eagle—*pathei mathos*. We are wont to say of a situation the significance of which others do not understand, "You had to be there." To understand who he is, Orestes has to be there—in body; and this occurs not over time but in a moment. It is therefore recounted as having been experienced in the aorist. There are apparently two sorts of presence then, and so Orestes replies to Electra's lyric at 1236 with "We are present."

Electra swears by Artemis (who, as hunter and virgin, is not the most "womanly" of the goddesses) that she will not be a superfluous burden in their joint enterprise—she will not be a superfluous burden by remaining inside (1241). To stay inside is, of course, the practice of women; Electra has decided to act, to be manly, and no longer to restrict her behavior to inner *pathos*. Orestes confirms her turn to manliness by reminding her that, she knows well that women too have Ares within (1243–44). He calls on her to remember that Clytemnestra too is dangerous, and by doing so reminds her of the constant, ongoing character of the ills that plague them. The question then is how to mix this ongoing need with the need to act now. It is no accident that the remainder of the play contains so may exhortations to stop dawdling and act (for example, 1288–92, 1326–38, 1367–75, 1484–90). Orestes ends the strophe by sharpening the problem; he makes explicit that the needs that ever plague them must be made present (1251–52).

Electra begins the antistrophe (1253–72) by reiterating and so emphasizing the difficulty of their situation. The presence of all time justifies speaking out, but only with difficulty does her mouth speak now (1253–56). All time, and so any time, is the time for justice. We must look to the pattern of right to justify any particular enactment of right. But such justification is strange (it frees the mouth with difficulty) because on the one hand it justifies specific acts of retribution (for example, killing Clytemnestra and Aegisthus) while, on the other hand, since the justification is all of time, it still does not explain why it is right to do something now. Any time is not some time. Orestes glides past this problem, agreeing with and praising her freedom to speak while ignoring the difficulty. He urges her to preserve this new-found freedom, but she answers, "By doing what?" (1258)—she does not know how. Orestes answers her plea with, "by not wanting to speak at length of what is *kairos*" (1259). There is a particular moment for justice.

Electra has no notion of what is *kairos*; for her, every moment is *kairos*. This is why she did not understand why Orestes had not come (this is the meaning of the epode—1273–88). There is a connection between "being present," body, and action and the *kairos*. The perfectly opportune moment can be acknowledged retrospectively (it is of interest that the talk of past events here is in the aorist), but it obviously cannot be given a generic account. We do not recognize it in the past with the same faculty by which we would have to specify it in the future (interpreters of poetry are not poets). And even invoking the pattern of right, with its appeal to the point of view of the eternal, when articulated, requires time. And to say what is appropriate about acting justly at this unique moment, would take too long, an immeasurable amount of time. It is really inexpressible. This is the dramatic issue in the episode that follows.

The Fifth Episode: 1288–383

For almost one hundred lines, we are told repeatedly that it is opportune (*kairos*—1292, 1368) to act now (*nun*—1293, 1295, 1335, 1344, 1367–2 times, 1368) in the present (*parontō$_i$*—1293, 1306) immediately (*tachos*—1373). First, using the same word that his sister had used to characterize women who "stay inside" (compare 1241 with 1288), Orestes chides Electra for her superfluity of *logoi*. The problem, of course, is that because *logos*, any *logos*, whether for explanation or justification, requires time, it interferes with perfect justice by depriving one of the *kairos* time to act. Identifying, reflecting on, a time as *kairos* means losing the possibility of *kairos* action. So Orestes, in his own superfluity of *logos*, calls upon Electra to discover what harmonizes with the "now present time"—i.e., where to appear and where to hide so that they may stop their laughing enemies by their "now" path (1293–95, see also 1300). This will call for Electra to enact lies, to pretend that what she previously thought to be true is in fact true. Orestes warns her not to show her pleasure, to allow her countenance—her *prosōpon*—to glow (1297).[107] To this Electra replies that she will do what he wants, she will play her part—since the pleasure she feels derives from him, it would not be suitable to their present fate to do otherwise.

It turns out not to matter; Electra will not have to act. Only Clytemnestra is at home. Electra hates her thoroughly. Seeing Orestes enacting his plan for revenge will make her weep for joy, and Clytemnestra will misinterpret her weeping as grief because she never understands her daughter. One might say in Clytemnestra's defense that external behavior always begs for interpretation. What it means is never fully revealed to us and, in any case, since Electra is always lamenting, it would

107 *Prosopon* also refers to the mask used in a drama.

not be so strange for her mother to misinterpret her tears. Electra expresses her joy by saying that, having experienced the rebirth of Orestes, it wouldn't even surprise her, it wouldn't seem monstrous, if Agamemnon should be reborn (1316–17). In her joy she imagines that by way of Orestes' return she has experienced in the evening out of justice, the pattern of right in time. At just this moment, the two are startled by something Orestes has heard within.

The noise was the *paidagōgos*. His entrance exposes just how strange the conversation between Orestes and Electra has been. He calls them dull and without both *phrēn* and *nous* (1326–28). In their joy they have been talking long and loud right in front of the house where, should someone have heard them and gone to warn Clytemnestra, by way of *logoi*, their "deeds" would get to her before their bodies (1333). On the one hand, he warns them against *pathos*—their feelings have gotten in the way of mind. They must stop delaying and act now at the *kairos* moment. Here, the *paidagōgos* claims that mind and action go together. *Pathos* is the cause of their extended celebration of the fact that they have reached just the right moment. *Logos* about what is *kairos* has impeded the enactment of what is *kairos*. And yet, for thirty-six lines (1339–75) the *paidagōgos* participates in another recognition scene, Electra's of him, that reenacts the very danger he has just warned of. He and Orestes rehearse things that both already know (1339–45), and reveal his identity (1346–63) in a way that involves considerable circumlocution. Once again, then, recognition goes hand in hand with passion and with delay—something that changes the action not at all other than postponing and endangering it. The *paidagōgos* enters, he scolds them for their lack of good sense and mind, he tells them to mind him and avoid further delay, and yet his speech in the name of mind delays the action that was supposedly delayed by passion. To do away with this mindful delay would make action altogether mechanical, and so meaningless. It would be *anoia*—folly or mindlessness.

That Electra did not recognize her brother is not so strange—she sent him away when he was either a baby or still a child. By why does she not recognize the *paidagōgos*? She has not really looked at him; she has seen him only through his message.

You destroying me with *logoi* while having deeds pleasant
for me. Hail, father, for I seem to look upon a father, that in
one day I hated you and loved you most of all human beings.
(1359–63)

Electra once again experiences the pattern of right in a day, and so
serially, in time. By stepping back from events to reinterpret them, the
instrument of her pain becomes an instrument of her pleasure.[108] The
Electra as a whole is an expression of this strange combination of tension and togetherness, of pure atemporal being and ever-changing pure
becoming—a tension present for *nous*, for *pathos*, and especially within
the *kairos* as just the right moment is a display of the atemporal within
time. This is the gist of the response of the *paidagōgos*.

It seems to me to suffice. For many nights and equally many
days circle round the *logoi* in the middle which will clearly
display to you these things, Electra. But I speak to the pair of
you standing here that now (*nun*) [it is] opportune (*kairos*) to
do [it]. Now (*nun*) Clytemnestra [is] alone. Now (*nun*) not
one of the men [is] within. But if the pair of you hold back,
reflect that you will be fighting with others both wiser and
more numerous than these. (1364–71)

The mediating *logoi* that will justify this *kairos* action will take days and
nights to roll out. The *logoi* of temporal unfolding, the links between
then and now, will themselves take time to unfold. Still, now is the time
to do what they have to do. Delay for figuring things out means dealing
with those who are wiser, with those who will use the time to figure out
what you are about to do. Having heard this speech, Orestes says to Pylades that they must be swift, *tachos*, to go inside. They can ill afford
any more long *logoi* (1372–74). The appeal is oddly appropriate, for Pylades is the speechless actor. And yet, having been urged to act and then

108 It is as though she is a spectator of a Greek tragedy. Compare Aristotle, *On
    Poetics* 1448b9-15.

having urged it in turn, Orestes says that first they must pause to pay their respects to the gods of his father. Piety, our acknowledgment of the atemporal, too requires time, and must be given its due in a timely way.

Electra ends the episode with a prayer to Apollo. She asks that he hear the pair, graciously, conspicuously including the silent Pylades, and adds herself as a plural third "in addition to these" (1376–77). Orestes and Pylades, speech and action, are paired. Their single voice allows for unreflective action. Electra reminds Apollo that she has entreated him in the past, and then, leaving little doubt about how much she wants it, asks, throws herself before him, and begs for his aid in their plans (1378–81). She wants the god not to punish the wrongdoers directly but to assist human beings as his agents. This is the way to show human beings how the gods penalize impiety (1382–83). Human beings are to become temporal agents of the atemporal gods. Piety is apparently the resolution of the tension between the structure of right and the enactment of right. Having made this prayer, Electra goes into the house to help.

The Fourth Stasimon and Kommos: *1384–1441*

The chorus sing a strophe (1384–90) and antistrophe (1391–95) describing what is happening within the house. They do this while Electra is offstage for a mere 14 lines for the first time since 1–85. As a chorus, it is here that they are least a character and most an observer. They sing their "observation." Tragedy is, of course, poetry. Here its poetry is thematized. In the strophe, they begin with an imperative to the audience, "See!" What we are to see is "where Ares advances shooting out blood born strife." While the god's advance may be the meaning of what is happening, what we could see were we inside would be the advance of Electra, Orestes, and Pylades. In their way, the chorus acknowledge this by fleshing out the advance in an image, the dream of their mind (*phrēn*). Those who have gone within to pursue the evildoers are "inescapable dogs." They are now Furies—outer poetic manifestations of what is within. In the antistrophe we discover that this new role for human beings as instruments of the gods, is not possible without the assistance of Hermes who will cloak their guile in darkness. Not only gods, but their human instruments as well, show themselves only indirectly, as concealed, as mediated, as images. Presumably, this means they require interpretation, clarification. We must stand back from them to consider what they mean.

But this reflection is not what we get in the sequel—the strophe of the kommos (1398–421). Electra emerges from the house at 1398 claiming that she has to be a lookout for Aegisthus, but surely the chorus are sufficient for this task. Electra seems to use it as an excuse to avoid seeing what Orestes and Pylades are about to do. She does not want to be present. Being present is men's work (1398). But she does not hesitate, is even eager, to hear. Electra prefers mediated experience. What she first hears is Clytemnestra's cry: "Alas, ah, O house empty of friends, but full of destroyers!" This is more or less how Electra described her own situation.[109] Earlier Electra had in a way taken Clytemnestra's place (she calls Orestes and Pylades boys and claims to have been Orestes' true nurse). Here Clytemnestra takes Electra's place. When she asks for Orestes' pity—"O offspring, offspring, pity the one from whom you have sprung!" (1411–12)—Electra hears and responds to her absent mother, "But not by you was this one pitied, nor the father who generated [him]." (1412–13). Clytemnestra suffers; Electra is relentless. The two are not so different as Electra believes them to be. When Orestes finally deals the death blow to his mother and she cries that she has been struck, Electra sings, "Strike (*paison*) twice if you are strong!" (1415).[110]

Orestes and Pylades join Electra and the chorus for the antistrophe (1422–41); the chorus declare them to be present (1422). What is striking is how easy it all seems to have been. This is the ease born of the experience in time of the atemporal pattern of right, which may leave one remorseless and without doubt in one's own righteousness. The ease with which confidence (*tharsos*) becomes overconfidence (*tharsos*) is facilitated by poetry. Electra becomes the "true" mother of her brother. Orestes is "reborn" from the dead. Electra is so certain of her rightness that just as she had "seen" Aegisthus and her mother in her father's bed, she now "sees" Aegisthus coming from the outskirts of town "having

---

109 See 261–73 and page 15 above.
110 The verb certainly means "strike," but it is also the imperative of the verb "to play, like a child."

rejoiced" (1432–33). Electra is imaginative; she thinks by way of poetic extensions, presenting her predictions about what will be as observations of what is now. Electra makes what is absent present. This is connected to the nature of *tharsos* and its ambiguity as at once confidence and rashness. As it cannot be based on what is present, it is always poised to exaggerate and go too far. This tendency is built into poetry, which by making past and future present in the present approximates in the temporal now an experience of the eternal.

The Final Episode: 1442–1507

When Aegisthus enters, before he learns that the corpse before him is not that of Orestes, but is rather Clytemnestra's, he addresses Electra and accuses her of *tharseia* in former times (1445–46). He means she is insolent or rash, but his accusation comes, ironically, just as the bold plan she is a part of is about to succeed. She directs him to the proof of Orestes' death—his body. Their plan depends on this, a false presence—a body, to be sure, but not the right body (1452–54). When Aegisthus expresses surprise that anything Electra says could please him,[111] she responds that it was "by time" that she acquired mind so as to agree with the more powerful (1464–65). Presumably Aegisthus believes this because he wants it to be true. Both Aegisthus and Clytemnestra are "killed" while viewing a "corpse" of Orestes. Both are distracted from what is actually present by contemplating an image, a *phasma* (1466), of an end to their worries. Aegisthus says that the point of displaying the body is to make the Argives "obtain mind (*phrēn*) by nature" (1463). Electra replies that it is time that has given her mind. The corpse is brought out, and Aegisthus says "O Zeus, I have seen an image (*phasma*)." (1466). This is the precise moment that he is lost. His entrapment, then, like the long poetic speech of the *paidagōgos* on the

---

111 Aegisthus refers to his joy by way of the verb *chairein* (1456), and Electra responds with the same verb and a noun, *charta*, cognate with *chairein* (1457). All of this suggests a pun on *kairos*. Aegisthus is deceived by wishful thinking. He takes something to be *kairos*, perfectly timed, because it is something he would rejoice in, *chairein*.

"death" of Orestes, that by providing an end or completion in time, closure, substituted for swearing an oath—i.e., having the weight of the gods, the timeless to support one's temporal actions. The moment when Aegisthus puts it all together and discovers the true meaning of what he has "seen" is like *anagnōrisis*, the recognition, of tragedy. When everything suddenly snaps into place for him, Orestes calls him a prophet, indeed, the best prophet (1481).

Aegisthus is to die. Electra wants no delay. Orestes wants to delay. He wants to keep Aegisthus in suspense about when exactly the axe will fall. He wants him not to have a sense of completion or closure so that he can die at his own pleasure (1503–04). Aegisthus must experience his own death as altogether out of his own control. Full justice would require immediate punishment. The indeterminacy of an uncertain time is as close as one can get in time to direct punishment. Making Aegisthus experience this uncertainty in time is a way of taking his punishment out of time. At the end, in their very short exodus (1508–10), the chorus give voice to this view of punishment.

> O seed of Atreus, as having suffered many things, with difficulty, you have come out through freedom, having been perfected by the present (nun) impulse.

This experience of justice in the now is meant as a replacement for the experience of a timeless pattern of justice.

Nevertheless, one cannot escape the sense at the end of this *Electra* that something is wrong. If nothing else, the brutality of Orestes' self-confidence suggests this "completion" is somehow spurious and illusory. Put differently, if the main characters are right to be so pleased with themselves at the end of the play, why is it a tragedy? In the *Libation Bearers*, Orestes exits at the end pursued by the furies; all is clearly not yet right in the House of Atreus. Here things are different. As the issue of the play becomes one of punishing the crimes of murder and adultery, the problem of matricide, the suppression of the female, recedes from view. Clytemnestra does plead with the one she bore to pity her, the one who bore him, but emerging from the house directly after killing his mother, when Electra asks him how things turned out, Orestes replies without hesitation, "In the house, beautifully, if Apollo prophesied beautifully." (1425). He has no regrets—no Furies. Justice has been served perfectly, but where justice has been so perfectly served, reality has been replaced by poetry.

Chapter 3
Euripides: Electra Unbound

Puzzles

While Aeschylus's *Libation Bearers* and Sophocles' *Electra* differ in a number of ways, they are akin in making Orestes the primary agent of vengeance. As we have seen, Electra drops out altogether halfway through the *Libation Bearers* and, while her suffering is thematic throughout in the version of Sophocles, she is curiously insulated from the action of the play, which would not change at all were she not present. By comparison, the dominance of the agency of Electra and the changes it effects in both plot and tone make Euripides' version stand apart.

Moreover, Euripides' *Electra* begins with a prologue by an altogether new character—the "husband" to whom Aegisthus has married Electra off. He is an *autourgos*—a self-employed farmer. Now, while he is certainly more complicated than he first seems, roughly speaking, this nameless man is presented as good beyond anyone's expectation. He has not consummated his marriage—perhaps because he does not recognize Aegisthus's authority, perhaps because he is afraid of Orestes—but, in either case, the result is a marriage in name only. Neither he nor Electra accept the ritual they have undergone as indicating a real marriage. Electra is married to "no one." Euripides' *Electra* thus begins with characters who, in treating a *nomos* (law, custom, or convention) as a mere *nomos*, defy convention. In this way, Euripides begins with the tension that grounds all philosophic questioning. As in the other two plays, this *Electra* is concerned with the primacy of the female, but by way of the wedding of nature (*phusis*) and convention (*nomos*).

The distinction between *nomos* and *phusis* is both underlined and made problematic by the status of the *autourgos*, who is throughout the play anonymous—he has literally made no name for himself. He was chosen to be Electra's husband because he is a nobody; he is weak (*asthenēs*, 39), and so presumably could not generate sons sufficiently strong to be of danger to Aegisthus. This suggests a certain natural determinism—because he is lowborn, neither he nor those bred from him are a threat. And yet the *autourgos* is discovered by Orestes and Electra to be a *gennaios anēr*, a wellborn man (262). On the one hand, then, that nature trumps convention means that blood breeds true. On the other hand, it means that one can never trust a conventional hierarchy to reflect the natural order.[112]

Let us turn for a moment to the very end of the play. Castor, one of the Dioscuri, the brothers (now stars in heaven, 990–992) of Clytemnestra and Helen, is addressing Orestes.

> But henceforth it is necessary to do
> What both Fates and Zeus ordained for you.
> On the one hand, give Electra to Pylades as wife in his house,
> and, on the other, you leave Argos.
> For it is not for you to step foot
> in this city, having killed your mother. (1247–51)

Now, Electra announces early in the play that having been forced to leave home is a great trial for her (207–10). In addition, she has had no children because

> . . . this [is] shameful, for a woman
> to rule over the household, and not the man. And I hate also those
> children, whoever [of them] in the city has not been named
> from the father, but from the mother.
> For, of one marrying in a distinguished way and to a greater marriage bed,
> there is no talk (*logos*) of the man, but of the woman. (932–37)

At the behest of Castor, Electra will be betrothed to Pylades, who neither says nor does anything in the play (he is *only* a name), and who is to

---

112 The one meaning would vindicate Agamemnon, the other Achilles.

remove her immediately from Argos, her home, for the marriage is to be "in his house." Is this really the happy ending it is meant to seem? Electra's marriage appears to be a punishment.

Euripides' *Electra* is a play about marriage. Its action is bookended by two versions of the marriage of Electra—one preceding the play with a husband who may be good and a real man, an *anēr*, but who has no name, and the other directly after the play with a husband who does nothing to show himself good, but who has a name. She moves from a marriage in name only to a marriage to a name only—from a denial of convention to the utterly conventional.

Both superficially and deeply, the whole of Aeschylus's *Oresteia* is about the power of the natural relation between mother and child as somehow greater and more permanent than the formed relation between wife and husband. Aeschylus sees that, while necessary to political life, this natural relation is always a threat to the *polis*. Accordingly, he concludes his story in the *Eumenides* by providing us with three possibilities. If the Furies are altogether victorious in their prosecution of Orestes for having killed his mother, the *polis*, the conventional, will be subordinated to the family, the natural, and so, in its way, be understood as altogether natural. This would be the complete victory of the female, the world in which family loyalty trumps all, the world in which revenge and vendetta prevail over justice. If Apollo is altogether successful in his defense of Orestes, the family will be subordinated to the *polis*, utterly conventionalized, and ultimately destroyed. Apollo points out that the very existence of Athena is a sign that, should he wish, Zeus could altogether obliterate motherhood.[113] This would be the annihilation of the female—the complete victory of the male. And then there is the solution of Athena—the goddess whose only parent is a father. Her vote creates a tie. The issue is decided in favor of the defendant as the charge against him has not been proven.[114] True, the Furies lose, but by the thinnest and least insulting margin possible. Athena then convinces them (and so indirectly also Clytemnestra, who has lived on furiously as a dream within them driving them since the outset of the play) to dwell concealed beneath Athens and to become

113 *Eumenides*, 657–66.
114 See *Eumenides*, 734–51

the patron deities of marriage. They are no longer to be *erinues*, Furies, but rather *eumenides*, good spirits—their wild and natural anger tamed and civilized. To honor marriage is to honor an institution, a *nomos*, as legally sanctioning or legitimizing what must happen in any case by nature.[115] To think through the significance of this reaffirmation of the natural by way of the conventional, Euripides' *Electra* asks what it means for marriage to be the most natural, and so in a way the deepest and most fundamental, of the conventions of the *polis*. What happens when the natural relation between male and female is systematized by convention?

The action of this *Electra* seems at first to drive us to the conclusion that ritual or *nomos* is not important—it is at best something to be manipulated. The female triumphs. So, on the one hand, Electra's first marriage is ignored and treated as though it were not real and its ritual insignificant; Aegisthus is killed while he is in the middle of performing a sacrifice—his piety is taken as an opportunity to catch him unawares (774–858); and Clytemnestra is killed after having been lured to Electra's home on the pretense that she was attending the "christening" of a newly born grandchild (651–60). And yet, on the other hand, the whole action of the play depends on accepting without question a certain *nomos*—the custom of naming or identifying a child through the male line. Aegisthus' mistake is to think his safety will be secured by refusing to allow Electra to marry someone who is noble or "well-born" as though, even if nature were all powerful and blood were to breed true, the relevant blood is, conveniently and conventionally, solely the male blood. By itself, female lineage is taken to be altogether insignificant. And yet, unlike Aeschylus and Sophocles, Euripides makes Electra the mastermind of his plot. She artfully manipulates a not very astute Orestes into avenging his father by killing both Aegisthus and Clytemnestra. Orestes behaves as though he were simply Agamemnon's child and not Clytemnestra's. Ironically, this formidable Electra assumes the primacy of the male as well.[116] As in Sophocles' version, Electra is much more a "woman of manly counsel" than she is willing to admit.

---

115 The Eumenides are also to be patron goddesses of the weather.
116 "I came to be from Agamemnon, and Clytemnestra brought me forth" (115-16).

These two issues are connected. The Greek custom (and, of course, it is not simply Greek) of tracing descent through the male line might be justified as providing the principle of a family's unity, but its consequence is that the woman of the family, the wife and mother, must always be perceived as a stranger, as coming from the outside.[117] What happens to Electra at the end of the play as a punishment is simply the ordinary fate of women within conventional marriage—to be in exile. And this, in turn, requires the denial of the female line necessary if Orestes is to think he is perfectly justified in killing his mother. It is at the same time what is involved in Electra's preference for her father and brother over her mother. Both assume that "breeding true" has nothing to do with the woman. In calling our attention to this assumption, Euripides also calls our attention to the fact that Orestes' vengeance is conventionally determined. It requires an unequivocal continuity of the family across time possible only when we ignore the necessarily dual origin of the family (and, of course, of every human being)—as though there were no alternative to the convention of giving offspring of a marriage the surname of the father.

Prologue: 1–111

That these are the issues of the *Electra* is immediately brought to our attention in a prologue that begins with a soliloquy by the *autourgos* (1–54), followed by his short exchange with Electra (55–81), and concluding with a speech by Orestes (82–11). The tension between nature and convention emerges in the ambiguity of the first line. Does the *autourgos* address the ancient plain (*argos*) or the place, Argos—a natural land formation or a *polis*?[118] And how separable really are the two? The char-

---

117 Accordingly, in Euripides' *Alcestis*, when Heracles arrives at the home of Admetus, finds the household in mourning, and asks who has died, Admetus first equivocates, telling him that Alcestes, who has given her life so that he might not die, is and is not yet dead (521), and then says that the mourning is for a foreign woman (533) orphaned in his house (535). The mourning, of course, is for Alcestes.

118 That shortly after (6) *argos* is used unambiguously to mean the city is Euripides' way of calling attention to this ambiguity.

acter of the female as by nature hidden also shows itself in the prologue, for the *autourgos* gives Clytemnestra no identity apart from the men to whom she is attached. She is first "the woman/wife [of Agamemnon]" (9), then "spouse/bedfellow of him" (i.e., of Aegisthus) and "daughter of Tyndareus" (13). The *autourgos* first mentions Orestes and then Electra as children of Agamemnon (15–16), but is silent about Iphigenia. He makes not the female Electra, but an old *tropheus* (a male nourisher) responsible for spiriting Orestes away as a baby. And, in a plot detail found only in Euripides, Electra is given multiple suiters, "the first men of the land of Greece" (21)—the whole story depends on her being primarily a potential wife.[119] Throughout, and this despite the deed of Clytemnestra and its echo here in the manipulative nature of Electra, the question of the nobility of women is treated as irrelevant.

The *autourgos*'s description of himself is also strange. He claims to come from an illustrious Mycenean family (35–38), but then admits that being well born does not keep him from falling into poverty and weakness (38). And it is because he is weak that Aegisthus marries him to Electra. But then how is being well born not conventional, and so uninheritable? The *autourgos* goes on to say of himself "this man (*anēr*) has not ever shamed her by her bed—Cypris is my witness—and she is yet in fact a virgin" (43–44). But, if we take his speech at face value, it shows that he is not in fact noble, and that he considers Electra's bloodline superior to his own. This, paradoxically, undermines his initial claims for himself.

The general point seems to be this. Orestes and Electra assume that their father is worth avenging because he is the famous Agamemnon—sacker of Troy. By beginning with the *autourgos*, the nameless, weak, and humble he-man, Euripides forces us to call this into question, for it is not so clear that the good descend from the good—after all Agamemnon and Aegisthus can claim the same ancestry. Nor is it clear that nobility cannot be lost, for example, through poverty. Nor is it clear that the *autourgos*, though weak, will not be more noble than those who are strong. Nor is it even clear that the characters in the play believe that conventional nobility is real nobility, "for many, while being well born,

119 See note 65 above.

are bad" (551).[120] But if all this were true, to justify the action they are contemplating, Orestes and Electra would need to make an argument for the worthiness of their father, and this they do not do.

Electra's first words are "Black night, nurse of golden stars . . . " (54); whether wittingly or not, when applied to her own situation, her image suggests that the adversity she has faced has nurtured her nobility, that the bleakness of the one has made the other shine forth. Accordingly, it is important to examine this adversity. We first see Electra laboring—fetching water from the fountain. She laments having been thrown out of her house—discarded along with Orestes in favor of the children born to Clytemnestra and Aegisthus. And yet, by her own admission, she toils not from need, but in order to display to the gods the hybris of Aegisthus, which seems here to consist primarily in his having married her off. Indeed, her husband urges her to refrain from this labor and toil and to revert to the way of her previous life—a time when she was nurtured, one might say, pampered (64–66). To be sure, Electra is cast from the house but, as this is the fate of all women who marry, it does not really single her out. It was, for example, true even of her mother, whom she identifies here by the name of her grandfather, Tyndareus. Of the "other offspring" of Clytemnestra, we will hear nothing more. They seem meant only to remind us that when Electra and Orestes succeed in killing Aegisthus, by their action they will reproduce in others the conditions for their own trials. The revenge will not stop here. In these and many other ways, Electra repeatedly exaggerates the adversity of her situation so that the golden stars of her nobility may shine.

The Parodos: 112–12

For her own selfish reasons, Electra will play the role of selfless martyr. When she first speaks to Orestes, still thinking him to be a messenger from her brother, she will enumerate the "heavy fortunes of me and of my father" (301). She will lament the sorry state of her clothing, her general filth, her poor housing, and the necessity that she work. She will complain that she must make her own clothing and carry water from the spring, that she is without a share in holy festivals and is deprived of dances (*chorōn*),

120 See also 367–90.

and that, as a maid, she must turn her back on women and so is isolated. Here, just before she laments this list of woes, the chorus of young maidens enter. They are certainly not strangers to her. They invite her to a holy festival (170–74). When Electra declines, complaining that her hair is filthy and that she has nothing to wear (184–85), they offer to provide her with a cloak (191–92), and, of course, she might have used the abundant water she carries around (while having been urged not to do so) to bathe and to wash her dirty hair. The parodos (112–212) consists of an extended conversation in song and dance between Electra and this chorus of young maidens. Now, while the house of the unnamed farmer may not be up to the standards of the palatial home of her youth, we see that the rest of Electra's claims of woe—clothing, filth, toil, festivals, dancing, and female companionship—prove false or hyperbolic even before they are uttered. The suffering they describe is metaphorical. Euripides' Electra is the poet of her own misery. In the parodos, she describes the murder of Agamemnon with an axe (160) and shortly thereafter with the two-edged sword of Aegisthus (164–65). It is not specified what weapon was used in the account given in Aeschylus's *Agamemnon*.[121] In Sophocles *Electra* (97–99, 195–96, 484–87), it is an axe. Here, with apparent indifference, Electra says it is first one and then the other. It is both; accordingly, it cannot be said unequivocally to be either. Because Electra is so poetically fertile, we are never sure how exactly we are to take what she says. The chorus share our sense of her, for they chide her for preferring to make a show of her grief, for acting a part to make a point, rather than simply praying to the gods for help (193–97). Electra is a drama queen.

The First Episode: 213–431

With one exception, Orestes is rather cautious when he first meets Electra. She, on the other hand, is strangely rash. While Orestes knows of

---

121 There is a longstanding and ongoing scholarly controversy about whether the weapon is an axe or a sword that goes back at least as far as Fraenkel's 1950 edition of *Agamemnon*. For a partial summary, see Sommerstein, A. H., "Again Clytemnestra's Weapon," *The Classical Quarterly*, 39: 2, (1989), 296–301.

her marriage (98), and knows to seek her outside of the city, he nevertheless feigns ignorance (248) and reveals himself initially only as an emissary from her brother. Caution fails him, however, in response to her fear that he might kill her. Orestes responds that he might rather kill others who are more hateful (222) even though there is none he might touch with more right (224). Electra does not question the propriety of these remarks, although they are surely odd coming from a stranger, even one who is an agent of Orestes; she substitutes poetry for reality, and so fails to recognize what is in front of her just moments before she begins to spin an elaborate fiction about the details of her daily life.[122] Altogether incurious, Electra accepts Orestes immediately as an emissary and abruptly elevates his status from a looming death threat to "most dear one"—*philtate* (229).[123] All of this fits the drama she has written and stars in. And so, within thirty lines, she will reveal to a total stranger who might well be a spy for Aegisthus, first, what otherwise she has been at some pains to conceal—that she remains a virgin—and then, most shockingly, that she would be willing to help her brother kill their mother. With the possible exception of the invention of the *autourgos*, this is Euripides' greatest departure from the other versions of the story. What was in Aeschylus and Sophocles delayed and carefully

122 It is remarkable how often in the play Electra fails to notice the obvious. For example, when Orestes' servant arrives to tell her of the death of Aegisthus, she doesn't recognize him even though she had seen him only a short time before (761–69).

123 Forms of the word *philtate*, "most loved," occur eight times in the play, three times uttered by the old man, who uses it quite appropriately (to refer either to Orestes at 567 or to Orestes and Electra together at 576 and 679) and five times by Electra—referring to her father (153), Orestes in disguise (229), the *autourgos* (345) the messenger she has just failed to recognize (767) and Orestes not in disguise (1322). For Electra, it seems to be a word unconnected to reality, an almost meaningless formula, like "like" or "awesome" or "Sincerely yours," that has infected her language. *Philtate*, which in Aeschylus would have been used to single out "the one I most love" here means "you to whom at the moment I am favorably disposed." This is the key to the play as a whole, which somehow altogether conventionalizes the story it borrows, and to Electra in particular, for whom words mean what she wishes them to mean.

clothed in hesitation and double-talk here occurs early in the play and is absolutely up-front. Orestes does not hesitate to ask if Electra is willing to kill her mother. Electra does not hesitate to reply to a complete stranger, albeit one who is now "most dear," that she is. Then, she goes on to tell this stranger the details of her story, details that she never thought to relate to the chorus of maidens who have befriended her. When asked by Orestes whether her mother allowed this mistreatment, Electra replies "Women, stranger, are friends of their men, not their children"; this is a most peculiar way to understand Clytemnestra, the woman who killed her husband to avenge her daughter.[124] But no matter, it fits Electra's story line.

In the midst of this meeting, Electra's nameless husband arrives. Although he has admitted having no claims on her as a wife, the two quarrel like an old married couple. He asks her what she is doing hanging out in public with young men. She tells him not to be so suspicious, tells him they come from Orestes, and then asks them to forgive him his manners. He says he supposes that she's told them all about the ills that beset her. Since she has said nothing to the chorus, her only other companions, Electra must regularly nag her husband about it. He then chides her for her lack of hospitality in not having asked them in. These two may think they rise above their merely apparent, merely conventional, marriage, but their petty quarrelling reveals not only that both are concerned about appearances but also suggests how much more married they are than they imagine themselves to be.

How appropriate then that in introducing himself Orestes should give a long and unwittingly ambiguous speech about the relation of nature to convention (367–400). He begins by seeming to praise the *autourgos*. That "there is nothing precise in manly spirit" (368) seems intended as backhanded praise of the *autourgos* for his refusal to consummate his marriage to Electra. He is not as bad as he seems, for the truth of a man is not visible by signs. It is revealed neither by property nor family connection. A man is by nature more than the external conventional props for his identity. Of course, this is all true as well of the disguised Orestes, and so his speech about the hidden character of a man is for us a not so

---

124 Iphigenia is mentioned only once in the play, at 1023.

hidden defense of himself. He too is an example of the confused natures of men for, like him, good children sometimes spring from bad parents (370), and there may be famine in the mind of a rich man and great judgment in the body of a poor man (371–72). And so, if one can judge at all, one must judge not by externals but by nature and goodness of soul (390). Yet the remainder of the speech (391–400) is strangely at odds with its beginning, for he now speaks of Orestes as the "child of Agamemnon" (392), who is presumably owed loyalty not because of his natural virtue but because of the very lineage just called into question. And then Orestes summons his slaves inside. Are they natural slaves?

If Orestes really believes everything he says in the first part of the speech, why would there be any problem with Electra's marriage? Why would he praise the *autourgos* for refusing to shame him (365)? There is something deeply hypocritical about this seemingly generous speech, something self-serving in the extreme. A man who is "somebody," but knows that he does not seem to be, says that one can never tell if someone "is somebody." But his model for being somebody is still to be the son of Agamemnon. This is an altogether conventional rejection of conventionality. We know this because Orestes says, on the one hand, that the *autourgos* is a man who would manage the *polis* as well as he does his house, comparing him favorably to "statues of flesh, empty of sense, in the market place" (386–88)—thus, unwittingly suggesting that the *autourgos* is perhaps more competent than the dead Agamemnon, who did not manage his family very well and lost his city to Aegisthus. On the other hand, he still does not fancy a nameless peasant as a brother-in-law.

Orestes' self-praise in the name of nature reveals him to be conventional. Electra, more complicated, nevertheless suffers a similar fate, for she has made up her world—a poetic world in which metaphor replaces reality. As we have seen in the *Libation Bearers*, Electra disappears halfway through the play, before Orestes enters the home of Clytemnestra, and plays no role in the unfolding of the action. And, while Electra's suffering provides the motive for killing Clytemnestra in Sophocles' play, she is artfully presented as having no effect whatsoever on the action that unfolds. In both previous versions, then, Electra is affected but effects not at all. In Euripides, she becomes the active force of the drama, but at a cost, for she is transformed into a character who effects her own affects. As the poet of her own story, she artfully generates motives that are no more natural than those of Orestes. In the *Eumenides* Orestes' trial for matricide is represented in terms of the deep tension between the male and the female, which, in turn, is glossed as a tension first between political life and the family, and then between the artificial and the natural. Clytemnestra defends the natural by punishing Agamemnon for the sacrifice of Iphigenia. And yet, to do so, she must become the "woman of manly counsel" described by the guard at the very outset of the *Agamemnon* (11). Apparently, one can only defend the principle of the natural conventionally.[125] Here, to justify their deed, Orestes and Electra may appeal to the "natural" relation to the father; nevertheless, to kill the mother is to attack the natural. Electra unwittingly imitates, not Euripides' humanly conflicted Clytemnestra (1102–10), but Aeschylus's more consistent "woman of manly counsel," the Clytemnestra Electra has invented, poeticized. This conventional praise of the natural has something to do with Electra's elevation of marriage: "You speak just things, but justice holds shamefully, for a woman should defer to her spouse in all things, she who [is] of sound mind. To whom these things don't seem so, in saying [so], she does not even come to number among my things" (1051-54).[126] This good wife, however, cannot be a good mother. In making the principle of indeterminacy determinate, the fiction that marriage is natural conceals an attack on the natural that would compromise the relation between parent and child.

The First Stasimon: 432–86

The prologue, the kommos that serves as a parados, and the first episode are meant to establish the theme of *Electra* as the tension between nature

125 Consider Antigone's appeal to divine law in Sophocles' *Antigone* (450–70).
126 Denniston and others give these lines to the chorus, to avoid having Electra claim that justice is sometimes shameful, and so, in a way, unjust. However, perhaps the contradiction is the point here.

and convention, but the purpose of the stasimon that follows is initially bewildering. Other than providing enough time for the *autourgos* to fetch an old man to serve Orestes a meal, it is not clear why this ode should be necessary. It seems merely decorative—fulfilling a dramatic convention. The stasimon consists of two strophic systems and an epode. In the first strophe (432–41), Agamemnon and Achilles sail to Troy accompanied by nereids. In the first antistrophe (442–51), the nereids bring Achilles his armor. The second strophe (452–64) describes the rim of Achilles' shield and the second antistrophe (465–75) the center of the shield, Achilles' helmet, and his breastplate. In the epode (476–86), the chorus describe Achilles' sword, and address Clytemnestra—reproaching her for having slain the ruler of "such spear-toiling men." With the exception of the end of the epode, what has any of this to do with the plot of the *Electra*?

If the first strophe presents Agamemnon together with Achilles on his way to Troy, it must occur directly after the killing of Iphigenia. In Euripides' full-length version of the sacrifice, the plot of *Iphigenia at Aulis*, Iphigenia was lured to Aulis with a promise that she would be wed to Achilles. Since, at the end of the play (1414–32), Achilles is angry enough that he is willing to fight the Greeks to free Iphigenia, one would imagine him to be rather sullen on the way to Troy. However, here in the *Electra*, a light-footed leaping son of Thetis is escorted, along with Agamemnon, by a dancing chorus of nereids and a flute loving dolphin (434–39). The mood is airy, not dour; Achilles is identified by his mother's name; and, given the plots of the *Iliad* in the future and of the *Iphigenia at Aulis* in the past, he seems rather too easily coupled with Agamemnon.

We initially might think the first antistrophe is a retelling of *Iliad* 18, where Hephaestus forges new armor for Achilles, but we soon realize this cannot be. It is rather a reference to Achilles' first set of armor as a gift fulfilling a promise made at the wedding of Thetis and Peleus.[127] This is why in the antistrophe the nereids are heading not toward Troy but toward Thessaly. The antistrophe, then, is earlier in time than the strophe. The second strophic system describes this armor. The description begs

127 See *Iphigenia at Aulis* 1062–79.

to be compared with Homer's description of Achilles' newly forged armor in the *Iliad* (18. 478–608). Perhaps the most significant difference is that the detailed contrast of the city at war with the city at peace (*Iliad* 490–605) is altogether absent here, and so there is no highlighting of a marriage feast (*Iliad* 492–496) and no substitution of courts for personal revenge (*Iliad* 497–508). In addition to the Hyades and the Pleiades (*Iliad* 486), two groups of daughters who have been transformed into clusters of stars, we are given a series of female monsters (the gorgon, the sphinx, the chimaera). The imagery on the shield of Achilles' first set of armor thus either suppresses the female, reasserts the elevation of the female to stardom, or presents the female as monstrous. In the wake of the sacrifice of Iphigenia, apparently women do not appear as human.

The reproach of Clytemnestra in the epode is strange. Can they really mean to praise Agamemnon by making Achilles exemplary of those he ruled? Isn't the whole of the *Iliad* about how unnatural and utterly conventional that rule was? Accordingly, to establish the rule of Agamemnon over Achilles, the chorus must go back to the time before the war, and they must ignore the sacrifice of Iphigenia. In addition, while they praise Agamemnon for having ruled such "spear-toiling men," they do not describe men but armor. And so, directly after a hypocritical speech about the priority of nature to convention, we are given a choral ode that praises Agamemnon in a way that proves entirely conventional. In the course of this praise, the ode either suppresses, idealizes, or demonizes the female. Moreover, the ode itself seems unnecessary and present only as a dramatic convention. As an obtrusive example of an excess of convention, in not fitting, it fits.

The Second Episode: 487–698

All Euripidean tragedy is about tragedy. The *Electra*, no exception, is nowhere more self-reflective than in the first half of the second episode—its notorious recognition scene.[128] An old man, who took care

---

128 The second episode is in two parts, the recognition scene (486–584) and the plans to murder Aegisthus and Clytemnestra (596–698). The two are separated by a short choral ode (585–95) expressing joy at Orestes' return.

of Orestes as a young boy, arrives at the home of Electra. On his way, he has noticed that someone has sacrificed at the tomb of Agamemnon. Thinking it might have been Orestes, he urges Electra to compare the lock of hair that has been left to her own, to compare the footprint left behind to hers, and to look for any fabric that matches the material woven by Electra and worn by Orestes when he was taken away as a child. In other words, the old man urges that Electra reproduce the recognition scene from Aeschylus's *Libation Bearers* (164–234). Her reasons for refusing to do so mock that scene. Even were the sacrifice to come from Orestes, she says, the hair will not match, for the one would belong to a man bred in the palaestra, while the other would be the combed hair of a woman. Nor would the footprints match, for that of a male is much larger. And, finally, not only was she far too young to weave when Orestes was taken away, but had she woven his clothing, he is now an adult and could no longer wear it. What is the point of Euripides' abrupt and seemingly churlish dismissal of Aeschylus? First, with respect to the lock of hair, Electra seems to claim that what it has undergone is far more important than what it is by nature. Apparently, for this Electra, the true Orestes cannot be made manifest by way of any natural connection to his natural origin, his family. Second, with respect to the footprint, after initially denying that the old man even saw it, Electra denies that it would prove anything even were it present, since generic sexual difference trumps particular family identity. And finally, with regard to the weaving, Electra does not acknowledge that Orestes' earliest clothing might be a keepsake—a conventional sign meant to remind him of his sister; she will not even allow herself to be the principle according to which Orestes is recognized. Orestes' identity will not be revealed by his nature nor by his connection to a female (whether natural or symbolic) but, of course, in the *Electra*, the two are really the same. Euripides' attack on Aeschylus is the counterpart of Orestes' earlier speech on the relation of nature to convention. The principle of this parody is that nothing linked to Orestes' birth, his genetic make-up, is allowed to establish his identity. This, of course, is to minimize the importance of the mother. In the *Libation Bearers*, Orestes is aided by his former nurse (*he trophos*); in Euripides' *Electra* he is said to have had a male "nurse" (*tropheus*, 16) who reared or nursed (*ektrephō*, 488) him—the same male nurse who once nurtured (*trephō*, 507, 555) Agamemnon. Ordinarily a boy is said to be nursed (*trephomenos*) only as long as he is in the care of women. Here, the female has been linked to nature and both have been suppressed in favor of history. The male has replaced the female.

The recognition scene that follows the parody turns on something else. Orestes says that the old man observes him as though he were inspecting the stamp, the *kharaktēr*, on a piece of silver (558–59). In fact, the old man says a god has revealed a dear treasure to him by way of a scar from a childhood wound on Orestes' brow (573–74). Not something natural but something stamped on by experience, not nature but character, reveals who Orestes is. But then why should it be so important that Orestes is the son of Agamemnon? If it is experience and not birth that makes us who we are, is the Orestes who was raised in Phocis even an Argive? That Electra understands this difficulty is clear from her relatively mild response. She does not give a speech of the sort that Sophocles' Electra gives (1282–1321) when she discovers her brother is not dead but stands before her. This Electra asks only, "Are you that one?" (581), and then leaves the rejoicing to the chorus. By contrast, their song of joy (585–95) highlights Electra's matter-of-fact response.

When, in the remainder of the episode, Orestes launches into a discussion of their plan, Electra is more interested. She cares not so much who Orestes is but what he will do. She believes he is Orestes, but it is unclear what this means for her. There is a difference between what one is and what one does. For the Clytemnestra of the *Oresteia* the former is what is important. Its sign is the relation to the mother. In his *Electra*, Euripides has made what one is problematic, while at the same time shifting the focus of what one is to the less certain descent through the father. Euripides thereby calls attention to the fact that the natural makes itself felt in political life in a very conventional manner. And so, Euripides' Orestes and his Electra are at odds with themselves; they vacillate— first affirming some natural ground for what they are about to do and then undermining this ground by way of the very reasoning they use to support it. They are engaged in a plot to kill their mother, eliminating the female principle and thereby altogether conventionalizing human life. Accordingly, neither will ever mention the fate of Iphigenia; Electra

can claim that women always prefer husbands to children; both
Aegisthus and Clytemnestra will be killed using as a ruse rituals that
have to do with childbirth and child rearing; men replace women as nur-
turers of the young; and hereditary traits are discounted as part of identity. And yet all these things undercut as well the relation between father
and children. Accordingly, Orestes and Electra really have nothing in
common and are suspicious of one another; both seem primarily concerned with their conventional status. Insofar as they consider their father at all, they ground their elevated estimation of him on the status of
a man whom he did rule, but nevertheless a man who is famous for having despised him. And it is not even the man they praise, but the splendor
of his armor. Euripides' explicit debunking of Aeschylus, then, has to
do with a disagreement over the extent to which the natural can be tamed
so as to make it the ground of the political. What marriage gives with
one hand, it withdraws with the other, for what stabilizes political life
from without, because it is apart from political life, also inevitably dis-
rupts it.

In response to Electra's "Are you that one?" (581), Orestes replies
that he is only her ally.[129] Either the snare he sets will succeed, or the
unjust things will be placed above justice, and one ought no longer be
led by gods. So, Orestes is nothing but what he will do. The old man
says that, since Orestes has no *philoi*, friends or kin, from whom to
expect help, his success will depend altogether on his own hand and
on chance (610). Apparently, there is no room for the gods as causes.
Having already conditioned his belief in the gods on the success of his
own deeds, Orestes seems to agree. Now, while the success of the murder plan depends on the fact *that* Aegisthus is performing a ritual not
on *what* it is, still, Orestes first assumes the ritual is for the sake either

---

129 The passage also, perhaps even more easily, might be translated "I alone
am an ally." The sentence as I have translated it should be compared to the
beginning of Aeschylus's *Libation Bearers* where, as we have seen, Electra
first prays that Orestes will come home (138) and, shortly after, that one
will come to avenge the death of Agamemnon by killing his killers justly
in retribution (143–44). That she does not automatically equate the two
means that Orestes is for her more than, and perhaps not even, an avenger,
and so is more to her than what he does.

of the nurture of children or of a birth to come (626).[130] And Electra
plans to draw her mother into a trap by announcing that that she has
recently born a son.[131] Clytemnestra will be killed while on her way to
perform a ritual of purification, perhaps for the new mother (654), who
is, after all her child (657), or perhaps for the child (1124–25,1132–
33). In each case, then, the plan involves the misuse of a ritual having
to do with childbirth to facilitate a murder, and so the "killing of the
mother" has been accomplished already by the means chosen to kill
the mother. Aegisthus and Clytemnestra take children and the religious
rituals that pertain to them seriously. Orestes and Electra use this piety
impiously (which is to say, conventionally) to annihilate the principle
that grounds the conventions according to which children are taken seriously. They demonstrate this by praying for success to gods in which
they do not believe and to a father whose plight concerns them less
than their own misfortunes.[132] Electra calls the planned killing of
Aegisthus a contest, an *agōn*. This image of their deed dominates the
remainder of the play.

The Second Stasimon: 699–746

The chorus deliver the second stasimon (699–746), the story of Atreus
and Aegisthus, while Aegisthus is being killed. They sing of Pan, who
lures a lamb from its mother with sweet music. The lamb has a golden
fleece, and possessing it is taken to be sign from Zeus that one will be
the ruler of Argos.[133] This lamb is meant for Atreus, but his wife, Aerope,
steals it for her lover Thyestes, the brother of Atreus. Angered, whether
at the theft or at the adultery, Zeus reverses the natural motion of the

---

130 The old man tells Orestes he can count on the support of the slaves not because of who he is—none of them will recognize him; rather, that they are
slaves will guarantee their support.
131 Electra, who no doubt thinks that her mother would not care about a grand-
daughter, is curiously obtuse in ignoring the significance of Iphigenia.
132 Orestes names Zeus, god of fathers, and father Agamemnon, Electra names
Hera with power over altars, and Mistress Earth.
133 The sign that one is a *turannos* (710), king or tyrant, is a marvel stolen
from its mother.

heavens.[134] We remain in this state still, and so Atreus's recovery of rule is grounded in a permanent reversal of nature.[135] The chorus conclude the stasimon with a strange remark.

> He is said (it has little trust, indeed with me) to turn hot sun to change his golden seat for an unhappy human for the sake of mortal justice, but fearful stories would be a gain for humans with regard to the tending of the gods, not remembering which, co-generator of famous siblings, you slew your spouse. (737–46)

The chorus give an account of a convention that would ground all convention, a belief in cosmic moral sanctions. On the one hand, they do not believe it; on the other hand, they think it salutary. Their ambivalence is borne out in the immediate sequel, where they first announce that they hear a shout that points to a death, then think it may have been something else—the rumbling of Zeus as a natural phenomenon, and end by announcing that the wind is not without moral meaning. Having first doubted the significance of nature, they now affirm it. This is typical of them. They are prepared to act on the basis of a poetic fiction (here, the story of the lamb) that they do not really credit. They take their cue from Electra who, in what seems a thorough denial of nature, thinks she can hear an accent in a death cry (755). Apparently even death is conventional, an act in a drama.

The Third Episode: 751–858

When the messenger enters to recount the death of Aegisthus, Electra does not recognize him even though she saw him only moments ago. Does she not look at slaves? Yet she now calls him, as she had addressed Orestes previously, *philtatos*—"most dear." Noticing that he moves from being nothing at all to most dear to her in a matter of seconds, the slave

134 Compare Plato, *Statesman* 267c5-277a2.
135 The chorus omit certain details (e.g., that Atreus punishes Thyestes by feeding him his children and Aerope by throwing her into the sea) for the sake of focusing on adultery as the cause of Zeus's anger.

is a little miffed. For Electra he is the role he performs for her—no more, no less. She wants him to relate to her the rhythm or temporal pace (*rhuthmos*, 772) of the murder, not of Aegisthus, but of "Thyestes' son" (773). Aegisthus too is an event, what has unfolded. It is not sufficient for Electra to hear a report of Aegisthus's death. She must "see" the drama of the murder played out in time. This is not the Electra of Sophocles, who runs from the house to avoid being a spectator of the deed.

We wonder at the Messenger's story. The villain Aegisthus behaves with perfect propriety, invites the "Thessalian stranger," Orestes, to participate in the sacrifice he is conducting and even generously offers to let him display his skill in cutting up the bull, a skill for which the Thessalians are famous. Orestes, on the other hand, is not so authentic. He artfully conceals his true intent by pretending to be a foreigner.[136] He lies about being on the way to sacrifice to Zeus and about having been previously cleansed for the sacrifice, impiously using the gods as a cover for what he is about to do. Dissembling, whether by mumbling or by uttering them in a foreign accent, Orestes says prayers contrary to those of Aegisthus. In a show of his Thessalian skill, he replaces his sword with a cleaver suitable for butchering, not for facing a foe in battle, and kills Aegisthus as though he were a sacrificial animal. Orestes is saved from reprisal neither owing to any manliness on his part nor by his name. When the messenger reports that after the murder both Orestes and Pylades "stood fast," and then "he spoke" claiming to be Orestes (846–55), it clear that he means to say it was Orestes who spoke, but grammatically the speaker also might have been the notoriously silent Pylades. That we don't know who spoke is meant to indicate that neither do the slaves to whom he spoke. They hold off, but are spared only because someone in the crowd recognizes him, recognizes his body.[137] Orestes employs elaborate artifice, but in the end, he is saved only by something he could not have predicted, and so something for which he could not have planned.

---

136 Of course, perhaps he is pretending to himself that he is really an Argive. His accent and his manners have been formed by living virtually his whole life in Phocis, in northern Greece. He is almost as little Argive as George I was English.

137 This makes Electra's non-recognition even more puzzling. What does it mean that she never recognizes anyone?

*The Third Stasimon (*kommos*): 859–79*

The *kommos* that serves as the third stasimon confirms the artificiality emphasized in the third episode. In the strophe (859–65), the chorus tell Electra to "put her step in dance (*choron*)" and "sing a beautiful victory ode with their dance (*chorōi*)." It is as though they say "Look at us; we are a chorus." They compare Orestes' deed to the triumphs of athletes at the Olympic games—a real struggle is given meaning by being compared to an artificial struggle. Football is not like war; war is like football. Electra replies (866–72) first by invoking the cosmic gods—sun, earth (*gaia*), and night—and then says she will celebrate Aegisthus's death (not because it avenges Agamemnon but because it sets her free) by bringing out previously concealed ornaments for her hair (confirming the falsity of the previous description of her trials), and by crowning Orestes as victor (agreeing with the chorus's comparison to the games). Electra's first thought, as usual, is for herself— she might have said "Aegisthus is dead; now I can finally change roles in this drama."[138]

In the antistrophe (873–79), after again breaking the fourth wall of the drama to call attention to "our choral dance" (*to hameteron . . . choreuma philon*, 874–75) that is loved by the Muses, the chorus rejoice that once more "our dear kings" (*hameteroi . . . philoi basilēes*, 876–77) exercise rule over the land (*gaia*, 877). So, eleven lines after Electra had invoked *gaia* as cosmic deity, the goddess gets poetically turned into dirt. And there is a pun as well. *Hameteron* and *hameteroi* sound like *ametron*—"without measure." The chorus playfully hint that unmetric dance is dear to the Muses and that the old, dear kings are somehow unmetric—unpoetic. The stasimon is a poetic praise of the unpoetic.

The Fourth Episode: 880–1146

As Orestes and Pylades reenter, Electra echoes this appeal to artificiality; she praises Orestes by comparing his having killed Aegisthus to having run in a contest (883–85) and Pylades for having an equal part in the contest (888–89). And in response, Orestes all but collapses the gods

138 See also 911 and 957.

into chance (890, 892). He claims that he killed Aegisthus by deeds not by speeches, and yet by giving the head of their enemy to Electra, he makes it a symbol—almost a *logos*. From all of this, Orestes unwittingly draws the perfectly correct conclusion that "we have thrown together an enmity with this one without regard to laws of regular truce (or, drink offering)" (906). This is what it means for there to be no distinction between gods and chance. Body, which is in its way the sign of the power of the particular and accidental, becomes altogether significant—as though life were an artificial event like the Olympic games or artfully contrived like a play. No quarter will be granted because one's enemy is pure enemy—a noun, not a person. The collapsing of nature and convention means obliterating the distinction between the ritual that distills reality and the reality it distills—between what we artfully use to understand things and the things they are used to understand. When nature becomes completely civilized, lawful, logical, it is rendered brutal and barbaric.[139] The "laws of truce" are no longer present. And so, Aegisthus's corpse is punished as though it were he, and Electra addresses it as though it were he.

Oddly, Electra begins her long speech addressed to Aegisthus's head (907–56) with an extended reflection about how best to structure her speech—about its proper beginning, middle, and end. So, while on the one hand, she seems curiously detached from her speech (treating it as though it were an assignment for class—a five-paragraph essay), on the other hand, she is curiously overwhelmed by it. That Aegisthus orphaned her and tainted her mother is the meaning of the death of her father (914–17). Electra wants to punish Aegisthus, and so threatens him by warning that he can never be sure of Clytemnestra, for a woman who once betrayed her husband will do so again (921–24). As Electra presents no evidence whatsoever that Clytemnestra did betray Aegisthus while he lived, she must mean to threaten him with it now. But Aegisthus is dead. Electra then tries to shame him for being defined by a woman—he is

---

139 *Nomos*, law, occurs only three times in the play—at 234, where Orestes is said to observe no city's laws; here at 906, where there is no law of truce with Aegisthus's dead body; and at 1268, where, by way of Orestes' trial, the judicial law that a tie vote favors the defendant is said to be established.

Clytemnestra's man (930–31). But, again, there is no indication what-soever in the play that this was Aegisthus's reputation while he lived. So, Electra seems to animate the dead Aegisthus by attributing to him her own anxieties. That it is shameful when the woman rules the house-hold not the man (932–33), when the children are given the name of the mother and not of the father (934–35), and when, with respect to making a great and distinguished marriage, there is no talk of the man but only of the women (936–37)—this is what Electra fears from her own mar-riage to a nameless peasant. She seems also to attribute to Aegisthus an attachment to wealth (938–39) for which there is no evidence in the play, although, as we have seen, her own poverty causes her considerable anx-iety. Nor is there evidence for any further adultery on his part or any pride in his girlish, cute looks (945–50). The same cannot be said of her. The anger Electra displays at Aegisthus's head is thus only very tenu-ously connected to reality. Electra the poet once more gets consumed by the fire of her own images. Is this the point? To treat the body as though it were the person by threatening the head of the dead Aegisthus, really means to treat it as something more than body—as though by itself it "embodies" significance. This is akin to a situation where the law per-fectly describes and governs the way things are and so where there can be within the law no acknowledgment that there is a limit to law—no acknowledgement that the long arm of the law does not, cannot, reach everywhere. This what it means that Orestes does not acknowledge "laws of regular truce." When everything is determined by a *logos* unchecked by reality, what gets said is an indication solely of the will of the one who speaks. This is the rule of poetry. Reality, its sole obsta-cle, shows itself in the resistance to universality to which body points, a resistance of which the mother is the poetic symbol. Accordingly, in the play that is about the totalizing of *nomos*, the mother stands as the final obstacle to be overcome. The *nomos* against matricide must be trans-gressed. Clytemnestra must be killed.

Electra does not so much speak as give speeches—orations under-stood as artifacts meant to have effects.[140] What is curious about her

---

140 See 907–12 and 1060, as well as 160–65, 247, and of course her exagger-ations about her present condition at the beginning.

speech to Aegisthus is that she uses his head to remember his actions against her, and this is sufficient for her to treat him as though he were still there—to reattach his limbs poetically.[141] When she tells him that a wife who betrays once will do so again, she is trying to make him miserable *now* by altering what was true when he was alive. Electra makes no distinction between what a person is and what a person does—between inside and outside. And she interprets what others do through what she undergoes or suffers—i.e., by what is done to her. She began her attack on Aegisthus by charging not that he killed Agamemnon unjustly, but that he orphaned her. Aegisthus is the actions of Aegisthus, and these actions are the effects Electra undergoes. Since these effects remain— she is still an orphan—Aegisthus remains. Electra is always play-acting, for in a play, characters are what they do—no more and no less. This is what it means that Electra leaves real body behind by making body totally meaningful. It becomes symbolic.

Electra had demanded her mother's death for herself (647), but here (962–84), when Orestes begins to have second thoughts about matricide, he assumes the task is his.[142] It is not clear why. Nor is it initially clear how Electra so quickly overcomes his new qualms. Yet perhaps both questions have the same answer. When Electra warns Orestes not to fall into unmanliness (982), she reveals the anomaly of her own position— she is a woman who speaks for manliness. She has lamented her marriage to an inappropriate man, disparaged Aegisthus as a woman's man, and claimed that the woman's attachment to her man is always more powerful than her attachment to her children. Electra and her brother are engaged in the destruction of the female, but as a "she" cannot do it, he must.

This tension in Electra is clear at the end in her confrontation with her mother (998–1141), for she is more the manly woman of the

---

141 Electra the poet reassembles Aegisthus as though she were a god restoring Pelops to life.

142 The manuscript reads *exaitēsomai*—"to demand for oneself"; so, Electra demands for herself the job of killing Clytemnestra. This is usually emended to *exarturomai*, "to ready" or "to prepare," in order to avoid the problem here—i.e., Orestes' assumption that he must kill his mother. But perhaps we are meant to see this problem.

Agamemnon than is this Clytemnestra. When Clytemnestra arrives, the chorus praise her for her descent from Zeus, her relation to the Dioscuri, and the wealth she has from Agamemnon's Trojan booty. In her first lines, alluding to what no one in the play has mentioned, Clytemnestra replies to this tacit insult by saying that it is all small recompense for the loss of her daughter. Electra counters that, as a part of this booty, despite being Clytemnestra's daughter, she is like a Trojan slave, and her mother is like Agamemnon. Clytemnestra is the sacker of Argos. To this Clytemnestra replies that Electra is no slave, and proceeds to speak in her own defense. First, marriage is not a right to kill, neither wife nor child, because family is not property. Second, Agamemnon used the ruse of a marriage to Achilles to trick her into sending Iphigenia to Aulis. Third, to protect the city or the family this might have been defensible, but not to sustain someone else's marriage when the husband can't handle the wife. Still, in the end Clytemnestra might have stood for all of this if it had not been for Cassandra—i.e., for Agamemnon's expectation that he could have two wives in one house. Electra, of course, understands this as jealousy, but it isn't that clear, for all of Clytemnestra's objections can be summed up in one: Agamemnon did not understand marriage. He treated his wife as property, as an external possession. She demands some measure of equality (1035–48); she must be acknowledged as a soul, as something internal. Clytemnestra thus presents Aegisthus as her sole option—the enemy of her enemy, and so her friend. Her claim that Electra was no slave, not property, was meant very seriously even if, ironically, she felt forced to marry Aegisthus for his use-value.

Electra's reply, that a woman should yield to her husband in everything, confirms that the crucial issue is not so much Iphigenia as marriage. Her long "free speech" involves a series of assumptions and exaggerations.[143] She assumes, with Agamemnon and Menelaus, that Helen was a willing victim, something she cannot possibly know and that Castor will deny (1278). She once again ignores the inaccessibility of what is internal. She assumes that Agamemnon was the best of the

---

143 "Free speech" is here *parrēsia*. It is the word the Athenians use to indicate the remarkable freedom of speech that prevails politically in Athens.

Greeks. Her evidence for Clytemnestra's adultery before the killing of Iphigenia is that Clytemnestra didn't stop trying to be attractive immediately upon Agamemnon's departure—once again an inference about the internal from rather scanty external evidence. Electra, then, draws conclusions on the basis of a view of marriage according to which a wife belongs entirely to her husband. For Electra, women play a part—they are wives or daughters; for Clytemnestra, they are more. This is what is at stake in the absolutizing of *nomos*. The chorus see that marriage is subject to chance (1097); Electra does not. Clytemnestra, who at once loves her daughter and knows her to be an enemy, gives a mother's response—"Yes, dear, but . . . ." She says it is a matter of nature that some belong to the males and some love mothers (1102–03), and then owns up to being not altogether happy with herself and asks why Electra is such a mess. Clytemnestra admits being internally at odds; not only does Electra not know her, she does not really know herself. Insufficiently manly to be an altogether consistent character, she may be a queen in a drama, but Clytemnestra is no drama queen. Electra thinks that she speaks of the proper female role. Women are what they are solely by virtue of their relation to their husbands. They are known as wives and mothers. She speaks forcefully of their proper silence.[144] She acts passionately in the name of their passivity. In her powerful advocacy, Electra dilutes the power of the feminine that Clytemnestra, less sure of herself and less consistent, represents.

The Fourth Stasimon: 1147–1232

In place of the fourth stasimon the chorus sing a kommos with Electra and Orestes. They begin with a vivid account of the death of Agamemnon. As they are a chorus of unmarried virgins, they are too young to know about what they sing directly. The time is wrong. And, in any case, as living outside the city in the boondocks, they are ill-placed. They have only second-hand knowledge, stories, poetry to go by. And when they go on to sing of Clytemnestra's role in that death as "taking axe in hand" (1160), their high tragic tone is strangely at odds with the scene we have

144 Compare Sophocles' Ajax, 293.

just witnessed. The mother who fusses about Electra's unkempt appearance is hardly a "lioness" (1163).[145] But when Clytemnestra dies (1165–67), suddenly everyone's tune changes. The chorus lament the matricide (1168) and wonder if there is any house more wretched than that of Tantalus (1175–76), Orestes invokes Earth and Zeus to proclaim both killings murderous and polluted (1177–79), and Electra claims to be responsible, having acted on account of fire against the one who bore her (1183–85). Killing the mother becomes killing "mom," but only for a moment. Orestes soon names himself a generic mother killer (1197), and Electra, lamenting her fate as unwedded (1198), becomes generically *alektros*.[146] Neither of the two can hold together at one time their inconsistent views. They are first altogether undaunted by matricide and then altogether daunted. In the *Electra*, it is the character Clytemnestra who is a "real person," for the mother stands for whatever it is in us that is not exhausted by the role we play. The mother is who we are—our natures—not simply what we do. That Clytemnestra had divided loyalties and so could not be of one mind is to say that she had a soul. To have depth means to be at odds with oneself. Effortless conformity to principle, identifying oneself altogether with one's *onoma*, one's name or noun, is superficial and shallow—soulless.

The Final Episode:1233–359

The Dioscuri, who enter at the end of the play to dispense justice, provide a symbol for soul as by nature divided against itself. They are somehow divine but with an indeterminate status. According to the chorus, they are not mortals but either *daimones*, divine powers just short of being unambiguously gods, or they are *of* the gods of heaven (1234–35). Castor and Polydeuces are the twin brothers of Helen and Clytemnestra. The story goes that Polydeuces was immortal and his brother not. When

---

145 The chorus's simile is particularly ironic, for in his *aristeia* (the scene in which a hero displays his excellence—it means something like "bestness") in Book 11 of the *Iliad*, Agamemnon is likened to a lion five times (113–21, 129–30, 172–78, 238–39, 292–95). The manly Clytemnestra who kills her husband is apparently still to be defined by her husband.

146 See footnote 68 above.

his brother is killed, Polydeuces begs Zeus to grant him immortality.[147] The request is granted, but at a steep price, for the two alternate in their immortality—one, one day, and the other, the next. They are the morning and evening stars—that is, they are the same star but appearing at different times and so fated never to be together. It is Castor who speaks here (1240) and says that, while the mother received justice, Orestes and Electra did not act justly, and that, while Apollo is wise, he did not prophesy wisely (1243–46). There is a difference between the actor and his actions, who one is and what one does. The Dioscuri have responsibility for storms at sea; they deal with chance—with what exceeds *nomos*. Accordingly, Castor cites a double origin for what they are about to mete out—Zeus and fate. As we have seen, Electra is rewarded with a suitable marriage to Pylades but punished with exile from her home. The *autourgos*, her husband in speech (1286), will go with her and be rewarded with wealth. Orestes is sentenced to play the role of Orestes in Aeschylus's *Eumenides*; he will be pursued by the Furies and must undergo a trial, but at the same time Castor assures him that there is no risk, for in the end he will be delivered and live happily (1291). Aegisthus and Clytemnestra will receive ritual burials. Finally, Castor announces that it was not the real Helen but her phantom image that went to Troy (1283); and so, apparently, the whole string of murders chronicled in the *Oresteia* was for nothing.

Orestes and Electra seemed for a moment to rise above the roles in which they are mere vessels for meaning, to break through the poetic world they inhabit. Then the Dioscuri arrive on the scene; things are to set to rights, but they seem instead to be set to rites. The *Electra* is, after all, a play. In the end, Clytemnestra only stands for the mother, and *autourgos* comes to be a name; determinate indeterminacy does not ensoul but rather creates a representation of being ensouled. Much of Euripides' *Electra* is designed to show us that and why "while you may throw nature out with a pitchfork, she keeps coming back."[148] Absent the limitations imposed by nature, the conventional is brutal. Still, at the end, the conventional reasserts itself, for we discover that even our awareness of

147 See Pindar, *Nemean Odes*, 10.62–90.
148 Horace, *Epistles*, I.10.24.

these limitations must take a conventional form—the Dioscuri, the two that are one and yet not one, are the visible poetic image of the gods in their necessary invisibility. Electra goes off to Phocis together with two husbands: the new one, Pylades, is "real" but is only a name; the old nameless one, while declining the name, is perhaps more really a husband.[149] Both are present, but nevertheless, like the Dioscuri, not at once.

The mastermind of the action of Euripides' *Electra* is a woman who defines herself solely in terms of men—father, brother, and suitors. She takes as ally a brother, but acknowledges him only by virtue of their common father. By manipulating Orestes into killing their mother, Electra conceals from herself her own manliness, her own attachment to convention. She pretends that she represents not the destruction, but the proper taming of the female. Her mother did not understand marriage. Any *Electra* will enact the murder of Clytemnestra to avenge Agamemnon. Euripides displays this vengeance as the destruction of the natural in the name of the conventional, albeit understood as the natural. Of course, it is all staged—a playful enactment in a drama. What the high drama of the play ultimately shows is a more mundane scene. Marriage can never be wholly successful; as an institution, it needs the threat of Clytemnestra to signal its necessary incompleteness. To presume its possible perfection is to presume that ". . . in the image of God He created it, male and female he created them" is meant to be understood as a solution, not a puzzle. And so, marriage is at its most natural when, while seeking to wed nature and convention, it acknowledges that by nature, it can do so only conventionally. The most serious of conventions is playful.

149 In the end, of course, "being really a husband" too is a symbol, a name.

Conclusion

"Presupposed: that truth is a woman—, how? is there not ground for suspicion that all philosophers, insofar as they were dogmatics, understood each other badly about women?"[150]

1. In their three treatments of the story of Electra, Aeschylus, Sophocles, and Euripides do the same thing, but differently. This may be a disappointment to those for whom they are thought to be dogmatics who would necessarily understand each other badly, and for whom thinking consists solely of eristic—of setting one view at odds with another in a contest to see which prevails. Aeschylus, Sophocles and Euripides are poets; their views are not so articulable as to be itemized in an encyclopedic intellectual history.[151]

Aeschylus's trilogy, the *Oresteia*, is reasonably understood to be an account of the relation between a pre-political vengeance (vendetta) and political justice, and so also of the inner experience of guilt and external legal guilt. The inner, the pre-political, is identified with the female; the outer, the political, with the male. That the tensions between the familial and the political, the female and the male, and the inner and outer are the same issue in the trilogy is clear in a number of ways. Clytemnestra, who is the only character present in all three of the plays and rules politically in Argos for the decade of Agamemnon's absence, is first referred to by the watchman as a woman of manly counsel.[152] This tension

---

150 This is the first sentence of the Preface of Friedrich Nietzsche's *Beyond Good and Evil* (the translation is my own).
151 Nietzsche's caveat about philosophers, "insofar as they were dogmatics," suggests that not understanding women is true only of a certain kind of philosopher, a philosopher that may not be as genuinely philosophic as we first think.
152 *Agamemnon* 11; see also 351, 1231, and 1399–403.

between female and male is highlighted in the opening lines of the trilogy's final play, *Eumenides* (1–33), where the priestess of the oracle at Delphi glosses over the conflict concealed in the transition from its origins with Gaia to the current authority, Apollo—a conflict between old chthonic female gods and young male Olympians. This conflict is made quite explicit later in the play when Apollo warns that Zeus could simply do away with women should he wish (657–66), and when Athena announces that, having sprung only from the head of Zeus (with *Mētis*, "mind," in the shadows as her mother), contrary to appearances, she is all male (734–39). And it returns when Athena, acknowledging that the success of her project, replacing vengeance and fury with justice by way of the founding of the Athenian jury system, requires that she find a way to incorporate the female Furies into her city, bargains with them to remain (793–915). These furies are, to be sure, hidden under the earth (and Clytemnestra hidden within them as what drives them, their dream-fury), but without them, there will be no justice. Aeschylus's *Libation Bearers* seems on the most superficial level to remove the female from view. Electra drops out midway through the play, and so seems to abdicate any responsibility for the matricide that follows. Orestes is now on his own, and so the female seems at first unnecessary.

But is it? Without the unasked-for help of the female chorus and the nurse who mothered him as a child, his plot would have failed. Just as the Clytemnestra of the *Agamemnon* had failed in her attempt to devise a scheme in the carpet scene (810–974) to gain certainty of her husband's inner motive for killing Iphigenia, Orestes thinks that by displaying the bloody cloth used in his mother's murder of his father, he can display her guilt. That he fails is clear when his inner furies pursue him at the end of the play. Orestes does not understand the depth of the power of the female. He is too confident that it is possible fully to disclose what lies inside us.

This tacit—half-hidden—theme of the *Libation Bearers*, the underlying reason for the disappearance of Electra, becomes more explicit in Sophocles' *Electra*. Electra is present on stage for almost the entire play. She does not affect the action—the killing of Clytemnestra and Aegisthus—but, as the title indicates, the play is clearly hers. In the story of her suffering and of its significance, Sophocles has displayed externally the problem of the internal. The theme of the play is not so hidden—manliness, womanliness, and the relation between the two are explicitly at issue. We are forced to wonder how it is possible to be just, for justice would require either that passion become disinterested (the task for Electra) or disinterest become passionate (the task for Orestes). The two (Electra and Orestes) are separated in the play for so long in order to highlight this tension. At the end, when Electra goes outside so that she will not have to participate in matricide, and Orestes emerges from inside brutally indifferent to what he has done, Sophocles, like Aeschylus, means rather to display in all its complexity the problem of justice than to provide its solution. His emphasis is different. The *Libation Bearers* focuses on the problem from the side of action, of the male; Sophocles' *Electra* thinks it through from the side of suffering and passion, of the female. But it is the same problem.

One is tempted to say Euripides' *Electra* is a different story, but of course it is hardly different. While Aeschylus gives voice to the female tacitly (Electra disappears), and Sophocles does so explicitly (Electra is visible, external for the whole of the play), Euripides reflects on what happens to the female, the internal, when it is treated openly as the cause of everything that happens in the play. His *Electra* is about the nature of the conventional marriage of male and female. It presents us with a solution, a wedding, of the tension between male and female, but a solution that, by virtue of its own inner logic, must fail. His *Electra* too is a reflection on the necessarily problematic, incomplete, character of human nature. All three plays first disclose to us our problematic natures—they externalize them. But next they ask us to reflect on what it means for us that we have been detached observers of this story—our story. They bring us to the brink of despair only to disclose to us what we gain from the experience of this brinksmanship.

2. Do electricians still speak of male and female connectors? Probably. The metaphor is apt, and most (my father, for example) would use it with no hint of lewdness or the subordination of one connector to the other. Still, it would not be difficult to replace, and perhaps it should be replaced. While *logos* is not all-powerful, how we talk about the world does shape the world we talk about. Electricians might do well to use another poem.

What about male and female generally? Could tragedians use a different poem? The slide from the eidetic distinction between male and female to the genetic distinction between real men and women as we encounter them in the world seems inevitable. This is the way of poetry. It sheds light on principles by embodying them and by making these embodiments exemplary. But by working so well, poetry risks working ill, for its exemplary bodies are best when they are powerful, so powerful as easily to be mistaken for reality, at which point the principles they are meant to embody are thrown into the shadows. That ". . . in the image of God He created it, male and female he created them" is a sign of the deep duplicity at our nature's core, nevertheless results not simply in the revelation of male and female principles, but in the genesis of Adam and Eve and their progeny—us.[153] Similitude lives only where there is dissimilitude as well; the cost of enlightenment is a compensatory darkening. And so, there is always something unjust about poetry.

We live in an age justly proud of its resolution not to discriminate indiscriminately. Long ago, Plato anticipated our situation. He saw that justice demands that human beings be treated differently only insofar as their differences are real and relevant to their tasks.[154] And so, for justice to prevail, we must think through what differences are real and what tasks are real. To assert that men are essentially active and women essentially passive falls just shy of overconfidently affirming that it is a man's lot to rule and a woman's to obey. Women have been to this country, and have no wish to return. For the Greeks of ancient Athens, tragedy was dangerous. By making its female characters so "manly" in their splendor, it intentionally threatened to call into question the conventional understanding of the difference between men and women. And yet the conventional order rewarded it, distributed prizes, for being dangerous. With us, ironically, Greek tragedy feels dangerous for a different reason, and we are no longer so inclined to think it prizeworthy. It challenges our view that there are no relevant differences between male and female. We forget what it means that tragedy is poetry. It exposes injustice while

153 Burger translates Genesis 1.26 as "And God said: Let us make Adam in our image, after our likeness," as the word for man here lacks the definite article. The plurality of God as well as the confusion between generic "man" and a particular man, Adam, has inspired a wealth of interpretation and dispute too long to be cited.

154 *Republic*, Book 5.

at the same time, and for the same reason, being itself unjust. We need it, but we must be careful of it.

Aeschylus, Sophocles, and Euripides use the distinction between male and female as a way of articulating what they see as the distinctive feature of human beings. It takes a variety of forms. We are conventional by nature; human customs and laws differ, but we all live by customs and laws. We have *logos* by nature; we speak different languages, but we all speak. Like all animals we eat and we have sex, but because we are the animals with *logos*, we talk about both—we make something of them. And so, our dining and sexual intercourse are inevitably governed by conventions—ordinarily different, but always present. We ponder, we chatter, we gossip. We are able to stand back from what we do, to take it in. We are always, if in varying degrees, simultaneously actors and spectators of the drama of our own lives. And because we at once act and observe, we are always in some measure actors—stage actors. We are born to be inauthentic. This would alienate us from ourselves were it not the case that to be a self is by nature to be alienated.

What this means is that the deepest part of our selves is always hidden from ourselves. We are ambitiously moved to organize our world, to give it form—we are rational and political—and, because we take ourselves seriously, we must take seriously the forms we mean to live by. We are manly defenders of the forms that define us—what can be articulated, ordered, what can be displayed on the surface. And yet, we cannot ever leave it at this. It is the nature of *logos* to attempt to articulate whatever it encounters, and so we insist on trying to articulate what grounds our speech. We want to say, after all, what we are talking *about*, what it is that gives rise to talking and moves us to talk—what is hidden and by its very nature resists disclosure. Justifiably, this seems to us the deepest purpose of *logos*—to speak of what grounds all speech, what makes it possible to speak at all. This task is at once necessary and impossible. *Logos* may be clear, but what gives rise to speech, what speech must point to in order to be what it is, must ultimately remain unsaid.

This deeper hidden ground is the subject of Greek tragedy; in the Electra plays it emerges as the female. Every human being has a mother. The connection between mother and child is undeniable; yet there is no argument, no reason, for it. Motherhood generates family, which there-fore in its turn shares this ungrounded undeniability. Tragedy is so pre-occupied with politics and family because the one is an exemplar of choice (we are free to choose our own pronouns) while the other reminds us that we do not make the world what it is by choice; we must suffer it—we are born into our situations. The latter—deeper, more self-aware, more philosophical, and of course, more hidden—is taken by Aeschylus, Sophocles and Euripides to be the female. The injustice of the condition of women, like all injustice, ought not be minimized. Still, it is no acci-dent that it looms large as a sign of the necessary hiddenness of what is most important, the truth we can get at only indirectly. A too confident articulation of this indirection will cause it to lose its character. When it is lost, we lose ourselves. Poetry—lies like the truth—is what we do; it is at the root of both morality and understanding. The injustice done to Greek women was real, but it will be our loss if we let this injustice blind us to the truth of their poetic representation. Morality is sometimes at war with understanding.

Index

Acknowledgments

I am grateful for many valuable conversations about the Electras and about the themes treated in this book with friends and students. I want to thank in particular Gwen Grewal, Holly Haynes, Stanley Hodson, and Emma Duvall. An earlier version of Chapter 3 appeared in *Nature, Law and the Sacred* (Macon, GA: Mercer University Press, 2019), a Festschrift for Ronna Burger. I thank the press for permission to reprint. As usual, I am most grateful to Susan Davis, always my first and most honest reader.